Crack the Spine

Spring 2015

Edited by Kerri Farrell Foley

This anthology is generously sponsored by Outskirts Press

ISBN-10: 0692507132
ISBN-13: 978-0692507131

Published by Crack the Spine Press.
Printed in the United States of America.

Crack the Spine Press
Houston, Texas
www.crackthespinepress.com

CONTENTS

Scrapple

The revolt against Harvey began in January after he forgot to log out of the shared computer in the adjunct office. Shirley Plato pressed the spacebar, and out of laziness, she didn't log out the previous user before looking up "scrapple" to answer a bet she had with Siobhan O'Connor about what it was made of. Shirley said it was sheep's bladder, and Siobhan said it was pork scraps—bits of pig noses and ears. After Shirley typed "scra" in the search box, it automatically filled in "scrabblecheat.com" from the browser history. "Come look at this," Shirley said.

If he cheated at Scrabble™, it now suddenly made sense why he was always telling people what obscure words meant even though nobody had asked him. Words like "weregilds" and "ranulas," words for Chinese coins, bones, parts of plants, and ancient diseases, words that always had seven or eight letters, it turns out. A lot of the adjuncts had played Scrabble™ online against Harvey, as well as the game's bastard brother Words with Friends™. If he cheated at Scrabble™, what else could he lying about? Maybe he didn't even have an MFA. Maybe that book he wrote was self-published. Everybody already knew he never made his students buy textbooks.

After Spring semester, Harvey wasn't asked to return. They let him drift away like so much detritus. Shirley heard he was teaching online classes through an online university. In the middle of the night that summer, she realized it had been haggis, not scrapple, that she had been thinking of on that fateful winter afternoon. In her guilty dream, she was pushing Harvey through a meat grinder, stuffing the bloody bits into a sheep's bladder.

Hospital

(for Esther at 102)
All the universe is full of the lives of perfect creatures.
-- Konstantin E. Tsiolkovsky, cosmist, father of rocket science

You were always so healthy
but things lose their way,
end up in wrong places;
even so simple a thing as water
takes a wrong turn in your throat,
enters lungs not stomach
and becomes an alien element.

Antibiotics beat back
your water-fed pneumonia,
kill infection running like deserting
armies in your blood,
but soon your clean blood
makes an oasis
in your stomach where
there should be water,
signs your stool for all to read,
and an ulcer is suspected.

At your great age
no option is good.
The doctors choose to observe,
give medication, not invasive
tubes, anesthesia, or even,
at this point, transfusion.

You can still swallow
but don't want the food.
You spit out the pills and the nurse tells
the doctor, *She needs something crushable.*

You say, *I'm so sad, I'm so sad,*
with your eyes closed,
needing something

to find the right way
to the place where your life is
confusedly fighting your perfect body
to find an out.

Captain Fantastic and the Brown Dirt Cowboy

He picked me up just past Johnny's at Fife, along a stretch of service road that ran under the freeway. He pulled up in a gold '68 Mercury with power windows, and *you* derisively asked if this was really the sort of thing I was looking for. But then down came the window and he was just so damned beautiful in that white-Jesus sort of way that even *you* were momentarily silenced. *You:* the incessant, omnipresent chorus of parents and teachers and other strident finger-wagers. So I slid my bag between us on the long, chocolate brown seat and got in. Elton John was playing: "Someone Saved My Life Tonight." *You* asked if that was ironic or corny or both. *You* asked what I was doing in a stranger's car. And then he asked if I was a runaway, just matter-of-fact. I told him not exactly, that I wasn't so much leaving a place as I was just maybe looking for my next one. Anyway, I was already too old to be a runaway, I told him; not a kid anymore. I unzipped my duffle bag and the head of my Westie, Toto, peeked out. Toto looked at the driver, who had said his name was Tom, and gave a little bark. Tom smiled and said the way he figured it, we were looking for a place to crash. A short while later we pulled into the driveway of a rundown Victorian with lights burning from every window. Inside there were others: some sitting around the TV watching *Barney Miller*; others alone in darker corners, reading or talking or eating cantaloupe chunks with chopsticks. Elton John played here, too. The album was just out – I'd seen a life-size cutout of him downtown before making for the service road. But still. *You* seemed to think it had meaning, like maybe it was the cold-blooded anthem of a cult. I told *you* to shut up, shut up and try and enjoy the fucking adventure and the warm house, and as I was thinking this, Tom kissed a girl on the sofa, a kiss with more passion than if she were a friend and not enough if she were a lover. Toto and I followed him to the kitchen where he offered me some sweet tea and a baloney sandwich; he gave Toto the half-eaten hotdog that was left on the table. We both ate hungrily and then he took us to his room. It was sparse: an iron bed with a thin white blanket made with hospital corners; *The SCUM Manifesto* sat upright, the only book on the sill; the walls were white except for the fine cracks in the plaster. I asked about the girl he kissed and he just said, "no worries, she gets it." I asked if there was about to be some sort of orgy downstairs and he laughed and that made me feel like an innocent. He said most of the people in the house were members of a band, living together, jamming, recording. Screwing, but not all at once. And then from another room, maybe the same room where Elton John continued to play, an argument: something about someone needing a change, which I could actually hear in their voice. It was hard to tell if it was two men or two women or one of each. Tom left me sitting on the bed; a few moments later the yelling stopped. When Tom returned he said we'd have to share the bed as all the others were taken. I told him I could sleep on the floor, I didn't mind, although I did mind and I wanted very much to share that little iron bed with him. He said we'd share. *You* said I was making bad choices again. I said goodnight. In the dark, Tom kissed me, and it resulted in a wet dream. Or, maybe the kiss itself was part of the dream, and the real kiss didn't happen until later. Time had a way of fuzzying just then, so that it was hard to pinpoint when was the moment when things really happened; for instance, when exactly did Tom and I became lovers: the Captain and the Kid? Of course *you* said that wouldn't last. But I didn't care; I basked in living in the moment. Tom said we were soul mates and that we'd been destined to meet. He said something forceful had drawn him onto that service road, to find me. *You* didn't buy that crap, just like you didn't buy his daily invocations of love, and warned me to brace. But it didn't matter. Because eventually, at the end of a long day of country driving in Tom's golden car, I asked him what he thought was at the end of a road up ahead. It was an apple orchard and we got out and Tom picked two apples from the highest branch he could reach. We sat under the tree while Toto explored a patch of Scotch broom nearby. Tom said he'd been thinking, maybe I needed to start finding my way out of here. I knew he was sincere and I knew what he meant even if I didn't know what it meant practically. *You* said he was giving me the brush off. But I thought he was telling me it was time to go home, just like I'd been feeling so deeply myself for awhile now, and isn't that the very sort of understanding that makes two people soul mates? I started to say something corny: "We'll always have Paris." Instead I just ate my apple and let myself imagine for a long time how nice it was going to be to sleep in my own bed again.

Sunday Afternoon

The whole week seems to turn
  around the axis of Sunday afternoon—
to pause even as it rushes
                forward into tarnished hours—
trying to finish, to taste, to gather—
  gathering ashes, tasting futility, finishing nothing—
    knowing that Monday morning comes,
      it always comes. A perfect hour
           is a ghost, or less, a memory—
that cold green afternoon in Aberdeen
  crowned by beeches, Tai Qi outside
the Chinese temple in December sunlight,
    your hand in mine as we walked beside a field
          of blooming thistles—Memory is less
    substantial than pain, the pain
    that only wants someone to feel it
          before it will go away—
  Sunday, meanwhile, perfects its sadness:
the smell of onions and laundry,
  a line of sunlight drifting slowly
  across the wall, sending up flares
where it touches some polished surface,
      then moving on.

Interstate 80

"Angela went to Albequerque, Billy went to Bermuda, Carlton went to Cicily…"

"That doesn't work!" Aysha yelled from the front of the pick-up truck back at her brother, "Sicily starts with an S."

"No it doesn't," Reggie replied, sure his sister was right. She was always right.

"S-i-c-i-l-y, I win!" she yelled at the top of her lungs.

"Ugh, not fair, " Reggie mumbled under his breath, settling in for the long journey ahead.

The family was on their way to the state fair where they were going to enter their pumpkin, the one that took six men, dad's plow and one small girl all their might to roll into the back of the truck. The rear tires looked almost flat from the weight and Reggie had a bumpy ride as each dip in the road made the entire vehicle lurch.

"Are we there yet?" Aysha asked growing sleepy in the front seat, the combination of the endless stretches of land and warm heat from the vents making her eyelids heavy and her mind wander.

Dad was silent. He hadn't spoken a word yet, two hours into the ride. In response to this most recent question, he grabbed for a cigarette from his front breast pocket and pushed in the car lighter, glancing in Aysha's direction only upon hearing the pop of its readiness. She was fast asleep. He lit his cigarette and cracked his window to let it hang out. A glance in the rearview mirror revealed Reggie was passed out too, making little unconscious grunting noises each time they hit a bump.

It was still five hours to town and the sun was setting as they drove into the horizon of yellow, orange and finally red. On the side of the road was the old familiar sign, "Last rest stop for 80 miles." He eased the truck over onto the exit and coasted down the woodsy country road.

In the distance he saw it, the set of red wooden bungalows with their cracked hand-painted sign, "Tim's Rooms for Rent." He eased the truck onto the gravel and put on the brake. He opened and closed the door quickly enough for the kids to peek open their eyes and grumble.

He approached 3A, a small bungalow with black hand drawn letters and took the key out of his back right pocket. The door, with a good firm push popped open, the last rays of the sun filtered though the blinds and onto the orange coverlets of the twin beds. He didn't bother to close the door. He sat on the nearest bed's edge, cigarette still in hand, and waited for someone to come in and find him.

The Moon Called Last Night

The moon called last night,
three fifty-one a.m. Full
to the brim—she had to tell
someone. When I answered,
she was speechless, perhaps
as much in awe of me as I of her.
Maybe she called not so much
to say anything as to exceed
her boundaries, have me
exceed mine.

Mr. Mason's Movie Camera

"Sandy, stop it! Gergo? Do something with them."

"Roza, I have to get dressed."

"Gergo, I thought you weren't going to work today? Is that the baby crying?"

"For a little—"

"Gergo, you told me you weren't? The chicken—I haven't even started the chicken yet. Sandy, leave your brother *alone*, d'you hear me? Gergo, this is *your* family who's coming, not mine. Sándor—I said stop that! Gergo, *please . . .*"

At night the skies over Ganaego trembled like a lamp whose bulb had come loose in its socket. In the passageways between the parallel banks of row houses, orange and green shadows wobbled against the wood, and grains of fly ash blew across our shared porches. *Black sugar,* Papa called it, and for a long time that perplexed me. You could always smell the steelworks. A limestone and burned match odor that clung to your clothes and followed you indoors from room to room. And you could always hear it: the hoarse bellow rising from the throats of the Bessemers; the piccolo chatter of the machine shops; the spit and fizz of escaping steam; and the whistle, more shriek than whistle, really, the imperious ribbon of sound that sent the men streaming into the smoky brick streets like so many flecks of fly ash themselves. When locomotives drawing strings of coal gondolas bowled down our steep-shouldered valley, the pane in my bedroom window hummed in its frame, and that awed me. And when Mr. William J. Pennystone, who shoveled that coal in the Coke Works and lived on the other side of our party wall, the only cake-eater we knew, tramped home, the skin around Mr. Pennystone's eyes that lay beyond his goggles was browned from the heat of the furnaces and so deeply imprinted with cinders, like grains of pepper speckling his pores, that no amount of scrubbing ever seemed to clean it. He looked like a chimpanzee, Mr. William J. Pennystone did, and, while that cruel mockery served to amuse me, so much so I liked telling my younger brother Adam that he, too, looked like a chimpanzee, Mr. Pennystone's discolored skin also awed me, as well.

But Papa, although he too every day went to the mill, disappearing down the street that spiraled to the valley floor like the mainspring of a watch, did not get dirty. True, Mama, bending over the bleachy washtub scrubbing the heavy cotton of Papa's white shirts, might not agree, but even I, who, at eleven, was never quite certain what it was that an assistant buyer bought, knew the difference between a smudged shirt and skin tanned like leather. Papa worked Saturday mornings. Today, before our picnic at Biddleford Park, the first family reunion the Kertészes had ever had, he scolded me and pointed at the car. "Get in," he growled. "You're coming with me."

"Yes, Papa."

At the bottom of town, where shifty men loitered before the cobbler's shop and a Chinaman, skirts flying, would dash out from his laundry to shoo away from his stoop any woozy drunks who happened to roll up there, Roosevelt Avenue truncated in a fork, before a tunnel. For the first time in my life, rather than bearing right or left, I sailed straight on through the tunnel—past the stony-faced guards with black pistols.

"Listen." Papa pulled in beside a large rectangular building. "Do *not* get out of this car, or you'll spend the afternoon, not at a picnic, but in your room. Understand?"

"Yes, Papa."

"Your brother has done nothing to deserve your persecution."

"Yes, Papa."

"Do not—I repeat, do *not*—leave this car."

Not a tall man, my papa, not pie-faced like Mr. Pennystone, not someone who said *Har-har-har!*—Papa had a needle-sharp nose and piercing eyes behind rimless spectacles, dark glossy hair combed so straight back you could trace each deep furrow his comb produced, and, between his ears, an *arithmometer*. At least that's what Uncle Alfred, who sorted mail in the Post Office, said, pressing the keys of an imaginary adding machine, yanking the tally lever and pointing his finger at his temple. After Papa, adjusting the brim of his mouse-gray felt hat, strode away, I studied two men whitewashing a wall. Their hats, their faces, their shirts, their pants, even their boots were so spattered with whitewash you could barely distinguish them from their finished work. Between the buildings other men on electric carts passed to and fro, silent as spies. I cataloged an intriguing assortment of sounds, pings, pops, clangs, bangs and thumps, and, amid this clatter, as though an afterthought, the fragile cries of men. In the immediate distance loomed the blast furnaces. Those I had no trouble identifying, no boy in Ganaego ever did: the enormous bottle-shaped cylinders whose perilous catwalks were eternally bandaged in smoke. Along the flank of one a little skip car crept up an incline. In the far gauzy distance towered the stacks of the coke ovens, where Mr. Pennystone, tragically fallen in life, was forced to work alongside Serbians and Russians and Poles. The Coke Works stacks, as thin as black candles, were each, this Saturday morning, releasing into the heavens their own tall dusky plume.

When Papa returned, he snapped at me. "Hurry up, somebody wants to meet you!"

It was to be a day of firsts. Never had I been inside an office building either. And although the cavernous rooms were mostly deserted, the dozens of desks lined up in formation and burdened with ledger books and papers, some with bristling black typewriters, were themselves of consuming interest. As you became more important, did you move progressively to the front, desk by desk? Maybe, like school, you sat in alphabetical order? Papa veered down a row and halted before one particular desk, no different from the rest. Hiding my disappointment—I'd hoped Papa's desk would be special—I attended closely to his lecture. "His name is *Mr.* Mason. Just say, 'How do you do? Pleased to meet you, sir.' Anything that fascinates you he doesn't want to hear about, got that?"

"Yes, Papa."

"Now, what are you going to say?"

"How. Do. You. Do. Pleased to meet you."

"Sir."

"Sir."

Following along, I rehearsed my speech. Papa knocked softly on a door, then pushed it open and shoved me forward—and with this I was delivered of another shock. Up to this moment, it had been my conviction that bald men were, by nature, fat men, too. This was a theory I had taken some merry pains to work out. To be sure, not all fat men were bald. Mr. Pennystone—he wasn't bald. But the reverse *was* true. My best specimens were my bald Uncle Alfred, who liked to stroke his tummy as if it were a beloved pet, and Father Pollard, who was as hairless and plump as the Hudson he piloted through the streets of Ganaego. This theory had never been seriously challenged—until I met Mr. Mason, who, when he rose from his chair, was, you could see, even skinnier than my papa—and Papa was a lean man—and without so much as a single living hair on his head. Mr. Mason reached out a huge hand. "This the hell-raiser imprisoned in the car, eh? Got a name, matey?"

"Sándor," Papa said, then went on to steal my line. "And he's pleased to meet you."

"Even when your daddy's Scrooge of a boss makes him work Saturday?" In Mr. Mason's cheeks red filaments gleamed like electrical circuits. Terrified, I nodded, and Mr. Mason erupted in a loud braying laugh. "He agrees! So I am a tyrant!"

Papa held out some papers. "I checked these." In his tone was conveyed more than his customary disappointment with me. "I was hoping for a little more flexibility on their part. But, all in all, it's a fair quote."

Mr. Mason accepted the papers. "Fine and dandy. And now, Kertész, amscray. I know you have some sort of important shindig today."

"My sister's coming in from Illinois," Papa said earnestly. "She's bringing my uncle, and my brother's driving my other uncle up from

Sutton. They haven't been together, all three of them—my mother and her two brothers—in thirty-one years."

Mr. Mason slid open a drawer in his desk and lifted out a leather box, a case. It was gray, the color of Papa's hat. Mr. Mason unsnapped the cover. Inside, in gray plush, rested a camera. "Got this not too long ago. I brought it in for you to borrow."

Papa shrunk back. "Of course not. We have a Brownie."

Mr. Mason pressed the camera on him. "It's a *movie* camera for God's sake, man. This is gonna give you something you're never gonna get from a still camera. This is *real life!* Now look, I'm out of film—Walt Pitzele carries it—but here, take the fool thing." When Papa continued to cringe, Mr. Mason, thwarted, held the case out to me. "Hey, since you don't seem to talk, maybe you'd make a better movie director? Whadaya say, matey?"

~~~

It was Grand Uncle Izsak who rescued us from the day's first disappointment. Ever since learning that the boy who sneaked into Biddleford Park and drowned and whose body could not be recovered had necessitated the lake's draining, Adam and I had pinned our hopes on exploring the exposed lake bed. Adam was convinced we'd find shipwrecks with treasure, but, if the likelihood that Spanish galleons once sailed tiny Lake Biddleford in Pennsylvania was slim, you could make the plausible argument that the town lake, rowed and fished by several generations of clumsy Ganaegoans, could yield its own plunder: guns, knives, bones, silver dollars . . .

Mama scotched those plans. "No, of course, not. Gergo, tell them. They could get hurt."

"But Mama . . ."

"Gergo, *tell* them! There's lots to do right around here."

"Mama . . ."

"Gergo, *please?*"

Izsak spared us terminal boredom. Not only, we discovered, was our Illinois *nagybátya* a ventriloquist, employing his hands as characters, Grand Uncle Izsak could, at will, pass gas, releasing his gas in staccato bursts to punctuate his characters' voices. That the other grownups did not appreciate Izsak's gifts only made it all the more hilarious. And then, sure enough, vindicating Mama, we did hit upon, not far from our pavilion, a trickling stream. And that for a time entertained us, too— until Adam, dared to follow me and our cousins across a log over the stream, slipped doing his rendition of the Chimp Walk. Landing in the water on his rump, he fell back, eyes wide open as a doll's. He cried, he bawled, Adam always knew how to get even.

"Settle down!" Mama scolded. "You're getting all wound up."

To my mother, the world existed as a place of sudden, unexpected malevolence: Cars were about to plow through parking lots and mow you down; televisions were about to explode and electrocute children foolish enough to sit too close; hookworms, lurking in the grass, were about to burrow into the feet of ill-bred people who went around barefoot. In Budapest, her papa had peddled witch hazel lotion. When no one could afford his lotion, they were forced to pack their belongings—she carried a little plaid valise—and come to America, to Pittsburgh, and live in a basement tenement, where, while they slept, cockroaches skittered over their legs.

My father, on the other hand, derived his authority, not from the threat of retribution from some sinister origin, but from sanctions delivered by himself personally: Mama invoked fate; Papa spanked. Tie removed, white shirt open at the throat, Papa lifted his gray hat and reset with the blade of his hand the single deep crease. "My advice," he addressed me, "is to take a deep breath. Trust me, you will find it a very long day sitting in the car. I have a proposition: Why don't you take Mr. Mason's camera here and get some nice pictures of the family?"

"Gergo," Mama interrupted, "do you think that's a good idea?"

"Yes, I do."

"Gergo, are you sure? That's not a toy, you know?"

"Roza, Roza, what this boy needs is a job, and I think"—Papa's penetrating eyes rested on me—"he understands that this camera is worth a week's pay, don't you, my friend?"

Earlier, the family had assembled themselves around the three honored guests while Papa took our photograph with his Kodak. Uncle Alfred's camera allowed him, he boasted, to take a time-delayed shot. Unfortunately, so long did Uncle Alfred spend fashioning a stable perch for his camera and practicing darting back and forth, that the group started to squirm and fuss. As the *kolbász* on the grill sent up spirals of smoke, Papa suddenly produced Mr. Mason's camera and aimed it at us. You could hear, coming from the shutter, a ratcheting noise, and in a moment of collective stage fright the family froze.

"Do something!" Papa commanded. "The baby! Somebody hold up the baby!"

Scowling at the expense of the film, Papa had bought but a single roll from Mr. Pitzele, who explained that each side was good for two-and-a-half minutes. To my infinite exasperation, as Papa raked Mr. Mason's camera back and forth across us like a fire hose, nobody did *anything*. Rigid as the mannequins in the Company Store, there they stood, gawking at Papa, or—worse—turning away, hiding behind each other.

"Just don't *stand* there," I hollered. "It's a *movie* camera for God's sake!"

"Sándor!" Mama turned to Aunt Gisella. "I don't know where he picks that language up."

Aunt Gisella delicately pried the meat from a bone. "What do you put in your chicken?"

"You don't think it's too bland? I make it spicy, it upsets Gergo's stomach. Your *krumpli* is such a *delight*."

Uncle Alfred inserted his thumbs in his ears and wiggled his fingers; my *nagymama* and Grand Uncle Balazs consented to wave shyly, then lowered their silvered heads and resumed their bickering over a detail from their youth; Amália, my cousin, squinting through her thick spectacles, held up her burnt sausage; Izsak, eyes popping, released a stunning, truly artistic *rat-a-tat-tat!* volley of farts, which the silent film, sadly, would not record; and, with the relentless whizzing of the motor, I had watched in despair as the first side of the film wound down and Mr. Mason's camera fell silent on the Very Worst Movie Ever Made.

"*Really?*" Aunt Gisella said. "It's the same old casserole I always fix. Me, I can't touch it. One bite of potato and the next day there it is—on my hips."

That Mr. Mason's camera was *Japanese* had also earned it, from the family, a contemptuous disapproval. But with its two complicated lenses, one of which was a telephoto, and its many controls, the Yashica 8mm camera seemed to me the most wonderful object I had ever been permitted to hold. The camera was made of metal, not bakelite like Papa's Brownie, and thus heavy and cool in my hands. On one side was a crank that unfolded; on the other side, miniature sketches illustrating different exposure situations and a clasp mechanism with which you opened the body. After Papa granted me sole proprietorship of the camera, I retreated to the outhouse. There in the foul-smelling dimness, I turned the spools and rethreaded the film. For my last birthday I had asked for a pocket watch from the G. C. Murphy. Using the watch to time my shots, I positioned myself back from our pavilion to establish the setting, then moved in on my feature subjects: Izsak, a close-up of his motionless lips beneath his woolly caterpillar of a moustache; Aunt Dorottya, enjoying her day off from the Tin Mill, hoisting her skirts to immerse her chubby calves in our stream; Amália, swatting with her badminton racket at a shuttlecock in fury. When Uncle Alfred challenged Papa to a game of horseshoes, I got terrific shots of my uncle directing the trajectory of his horseshoes by waggling his fanny. It was, however, when I was secretly filming the three old folks that I heard something not right coming from the Yashica.

Fresh from capturing my cousin Jan kissing his girlfriend, which infuriated him, I had stumbled upon the aged siblings. Stopping well short of them, I focused the telephoto lens on Balazs, then panned slowly—unlike how my papa had panned—over to my grandmother in the middle and on to Izsak and back again. I had, by this point, used a little less than half of my twenty-five feet of film, and I had resolved to reserve a few feet at the end for postcards of people packing up their baskets and plodding to their cars. But what I had chanced upon here was so spectacular—wobbly blobs of sunlight and shadow dappling these grizzled faces and these squinchy eyes alight with curiosity, doubt, mischief, sorrow—that I allowed Mr. Mason's camera to go on rolling. Even though my mother was, technically, first generation, since she, unlike Papa, had traveled here as a child, it was *this* generation who'd been forced to make the anguishing decision whether to abandon everything they knew and loved to emigrate. And the fact that in this clamorous and confusing new world they had poignantly lost contact with each other made this afternoon—this *particular* scene I was secretly capturing—so important. The longer I played the movie camera across those time-worn faces the more the certainty took possession of me that what I was recording was something that the family would treasure and that would keep us together long after these three frail people had passed away.

It was then I heard what I ought not to have heard: The film stuttered and stopped—far too soon. In the back of the camera a little porthole showed I had six feet left. I checked the windup crank. Nothing wrong there. The footage counter, had that malfunctioned? My pocket watch confirmed the meter. The conclusion was inescapable: The film had jammed, and I agonized. Quit here or open the camera, fiddle with the film, and risk ruining it? If it had been a matter of only two or three feet, it would have been an easier decision. But *six feet?* I returned to the noxious outhouse, opened the case in the heavy afternoon gloom, slipped my finger in, began cautiously jiggling the spools.

Someone pounded on the door. "Hurry up in there!"

My cousin Jan. "Coming!" I shouted.

"Com' on, com' on, you little twerp, I gotta go!"

Sufficiently respectful of Jan's temper, I slammed the Yashica's door shut, wrenched the clasp around, and the lift-up tab snapped off in my fingers. My mind in revolt, in total stampede, I refused to believe what had just happened. Clutching the camera, I blundered out into the dazzling sunlight, where my bully of a cousin lunged for me. "Gimmie that!"

I fled. Running away from our pavilion, I crossed the log over the stream and raced up a path through the trees. I crossed over a rise and followed the path down, running until I could run no farther, falling to my knees behind a curtain of bushes. And it was for me here, whimpering in heartache, that this summer day at Biddleford Park took on the freakish unreality that nightmares possess. Everything Mama taught was true: *Evil befalls those who step out of line.* Bent over the damaged camera, I tried—repeatedly, stupidly—to push the tab into where it had broken off, as if I could, with nothing save the power of my will, cause the metal to fuse itself whole again. The door worked, you could operate the clasp without the lift-up tab. But that was little consolation, and, in fact, that was no consolation, whatsoever.

How long did I stay away? My pocket watch would have provided me with that information, but, by the time I returned to the picnic, I was beyond caring about time. People were cleaning up, and, indeed, the perfect closing scenes I had envisioned unfolded before me: Aunt Gisella sniffing a bag and discovering it contained my baby sister's soiled diapers; Uncle Alfred spying a withered *kolbász*, rubbing his paunch, and wolfing it down; my *nagymama*, clinging to Mama as she hobbled to the car; Grand Uncles Balazs and Izsak exchanging baseball caps. None of it mattered.

"Where've you been?" Annoyed, Papa reached for Mr. Mason's camera. "Here, let's get that put away before something happens to it."

I felt, wrapping round my heart, tentacles of evil. "Papa?" I held out the camera. "It broke." In my other hand glowed the aluminum tab, warm from my palm. "It still works, but this broke off the door."

Papa seized the camera and tab and sank down at a table. "Broken?" In profound bewilderment, he examined the tab, then—as I had been doing over and over and over—squeezed it against the jagged edge from which it had separated. Huddled over the camera, Papa brought his fingers to his lips. "How the *fuck* could this have happened?"

I had never heard my father use that word. "It just snapped off, Papa."

He turned on me in rage. "It *snapped* off? I *knew* I shouldn't have trusted you! Go up to the car! You hear me? *Go!* God! *God . . .*"

~~~

On the way home, my parents argued. "I *told* you not to give him that camera," Mama said. "Didn't I tell you that?"

"Roza, I made a mistake."

"This could cost you your job, Gergo—you know that, don't you?"

"I know that, Roza."

"Then why would you do something so stupid?"

"I *said* I made a mistake."

"You don't give adult things to children, Gergo."

"Roza, just let me think!"

At home, Papa ordered everybody out of the car. When Mama reached into the backseat for the picnic basket, he yelled at her, "Roza, will you just do as I say? Take Adam and the baby and go in the house! Sandy, you stay put!"

"Gergo, the egg noodles will spoil."

"Stop worrying about the goddamned egg noodles!"

Ever since I fell down in the woods hugging Mr. Mason's broken camera, I knew that everything in my life was going to change. Papa, who liked to criticize other people's reckless driving, took the treacherous curves coming off Seventh Hill like a race car driver. We burst from the alley onto Roosevelt Avenue with its late Saturday afternoon traffic and swerved into the lot beside the Company Store. Papa snatched up Adam's discarded, still-damp jersey and wrapped Mr. Mason's camera in it.

"*Get out!*" he shouted, jamming on his hat.

He headed across the street toward Fischman's. Of all the stores in Ganaego, Fischman's Jewelry and Small Appliances was the store I most treasured. I would cup my eyes to Fischman's windows and gaze longingly in at the expensive black and silver cameras, at the shortwave radios with their intricate dials that allowed you to listen to the great cities of the world, at the folding leather travel clocks that glowed in the dark. But not today.

Papa rushed up to a clerk. "Is Max in?"

From the back out shambled Mr. Fischman, my all-time prize specimen—better than Uncle Alfred, better than Father Pollard. Except for a vigorous fringe of black hair that cushioned the tops of his ears, Mr. Fischman was as bald and rotund as a walrus. He was also tall, Ganaego's most famous jeweler, a mountain of a proof of my pet theory. But as now, like my idle window shopping, all my clever theories were swept away. Papa whispered, "I need to talk to you." Raising a shaggy eyebrow, Mr. Fischman led us to the rear counter. Nervously, Papa uncovered Mr. Mason's camera. "Can you fix this?" Mr. Fischman eyed the broken tab. Shook his head. "Have to replace the clasp."

"I *know* that! Can you replace it?"

"Well, sure." Mr. Fischman, ignoring the film within, opened the camera. "These little screws, see them? But the problem is *getting* one. My guess is they aren't going to want to send one to a schnook like me. You need to ship the camera back to the factory. But you know"—he opened and closed the door experimentally— "it works dandy, as it is."

"How long will it take—to ship it back?"

Mr. Fischman frowned. "This is Japanese, my friend? Weeks? Months? Oy, I really don't know."

Papa wrung Adam's shirt in his hands. "Do you sell these things?"

"Funny you should ask? I had two of them. They sat here lonely as stray kittens for six months. Then just last month, I sold one, and now you're asking about the other. Anywho"—Mr. Fischman blew his big rubbery lips so they produced a merry burbling sound—"one more I got."

"How much?"

Mr. Fischman's bushy eyebrows rose as if hoisted by pulleys. "You understand, this is a pretty sophisticated piece of equipment? You'd be—"

"How *much?*"

"Eighty-nine ninety-nine." I saw—*felt*—the reaction in my father. Behind his shimmering glasses, his eyes widened, his skin blanched. Mr. Fischman, on the other hand, looked like he was about to start purring. "We do have a convenient installment plan," he offered. "Very easy terms. You want that I should set one up for you?"

"All I ask is this," Papa said, his voice a rasp. "If anyone, especially the person you sold the first one to, asks, you never sold one to me. Is that clear?"

"My friend, for eighty-nine ninety-nine"—Mr. Fischman peered suspiciously to the right and to the left—"my trap is *shut.*"

Before we reached Oak Grove—where Papa had declared we were going next—he pulled off into the parking lot beside the German Club. "Roll up your window!" he ordered me. "First thing, we've got to see if it's got a serial number. You see a number anywhere?"

"Inside the door, Papa."

Papa opened the camera and regarded the number printed there. Furious, he clawed out my film, flung it in the backseat, then fell to searching the camera case. "Usually, there's a card you send in. You see a card?" Inside the sealed car it was warm and stuffy. I could smell the sweat Papa was producing. His hat was crooked. "I asked you a question! Did you see a card?"

"I don't think so," I stammered.

"I don't see one either. Wait a minute!" Papa flipped back through the owner's manual, holding open the last page. "*All right!* I didn't think he was the kind of person to send these in. Couldn't be bothered! Unless?—unless there was another one! Could that be? Could've fallen out. Did anything fall out?"

"No, Papa."

"You're sure. You're absolutely sure? Better check the new case anyway."

Papa rifled through the case of the new camera, sinking back in relief when he failed to discover a second warranty card. "You understand what we're doing?" He grabbed my wrist and squeezed it. "You better, you had *better* understand! When I said this camera was worth a week's pay, I was *underestimating* its value! If I tell Mason we broke his camera, he's not going to let me get it fixed. Ronald Mason—let a hunky do a favor for him? He wouldn't so much as touch a *pencil* a hunky offered him! So we—you and me, Sándor, *us*—we are going to try to *trick* him! And if he finds out—*ever!*—I'm fired! In two minutes flat! Two minutes I'm out on my ass! Now—*now?*—do you understand what your carelessness has caused?"

He cast away my wrist, and I buried my face in my hands, sobbing.

"Next," Papa announced, "we are going to examine Mr. Mason's camera. If there is one scratch, the tiniest nick, we are going to have to reproduce it on the new camera. Did you put any scratches on Mason's camera today? Quit your sniffling! Did you put any scratches on it?"

I sobbed out, "I didn't put any scratches on it, Papa, I promise I didn't!"

He considered that. "All right, we'll assume that any scratches it has on it now it had on it when we got it. Now, look at the camera, Sandy, *look—at—this—camera—with—me.*"

After inspecting the camera minutely, focusing for many minutes on each side before passing on to the next, Papa decided that the Yashica possessed only two serious scratches. He removed the keys from the ignition, poised the point of one over the new camera in his lap, then faltered. "The worry," he said, more to himself than to me, "is that he hasn't noticed the scratches, but, because the camera's been with hunkies, he'll look more closely at it and think we scratched it." The fingers of his other hand went to his lips, and he groaned.

Then he savagely gouged the new camera, twice. The second scratch, I worried, was deeper and longer than the corresponding scratch on the old camera. But I was too shaken to say anything. "Okay," he said. "Now, everything's got to go back the way we found it. Listen: When we get there, you are going to say, *Thank you for the use of your camera today, Mr. Mason. I thoroughly enjoyed using it.* You say it—say it, Sandy, say it!"

"Thank you for the use of your camera today, Mr. Mason," I parroted him. "I thoroughly enjoyed using it."

"*Again.* Say it again, Sandy. That's your speech."

On our way to Oak Grove, at Papa's insistence, I repeated my speech a dozen times. In Mr. Mason's driveway, Papa handed me the old camera case with the new camera in it. "Here," he said, "you are going to give it to him. Do you remember your speech?"

"Yes, Papa."

When Papa rang the bell, a distant reverberation of chimes pealed within the huge house. The chimes sounded like vespers at St. Ursula's when Father Pollard would shamble outside and bang the tobacco from the bowl of his pipe on the downspout. A lady tugged open the wide door.

"How do you do, Mrs. Mason." Papa removed his hat, revealing his disorderly hair. "I work for your husband. He loaned us his camera, and we'd like to return it."

The lady looked puzzled. "*Ronnie?*" she called out. "Something about a *camera?*"

Mr. Mason, clutching a glass, lurched into view. "Whazzit?"

"Good evening, Mr. Mason." Papa lifted his voice. "We have your camera."

Mr. Mason weaved toward us. "Good lord, man, it coulda waited 'til Monday."

Papa shoved me forward, the gray leather case nestled in my arms, and, in that second, my speech deserted me. But this time I knew I was required to say something. Squeezing my eyes shut, I held out the case and screamed into the enormous foyer, "Thank you, Mr. Mason, your camera was such a delight!"

~~~

A stunned silence took place. Then Mr. Mason, and then his wife, broke into loud, mocking laughter that grew louder and louder. Across my father's sweat-blotched face a scarlet flush spread. On the way home, he pulled into the German Club parking lot again. Terrified of the beating I knew I deserved and knew I was going to get, I cringed, hiding my head. But he didn't strike me. As my heaving sobs wore themselves out, I began to worry about his silence. *"Papa?"*

"The scratch—the second one?—I made it too long."

On his white shirt, under his arms, were dark half-moons, like the stains under Mr. Pennystone's arms when he wearily carried himself home from the coke ovens. To see my papa like this—hair tangled, face streaked with a tracery of soot trapped by his sweat, shirt stained like the shirt of a laborer's—made me feel awful. What he said about the second scratch was true, and I knew that. And though I knew I was never supposed to lie, I lied anyway. "No, it wasn't, Papa. It was very close, I saw it."

"Yes, it was," he said. "It was longer."

"He won't notice, Papa. I don't think he'll notice."

Mt father's eyes were downcast and lost behind his rimless glasses. He shook his head bleakly. "It's all right, Sandy," he said softly. "It's all right."

~~~

That night, I woke to my parents quarreling. I could not distinguish their words, but they were arguing over me, I knew, over the money I had cost them and the peril my reckless behavior had plunged the family into. After that, I heard my parents fighting more often, and I believed it was my fault. Now, I know better, but it was true that Mama wanted to punish me and Papa held fast to the idea that punishment was not necessary. All that year, I worried that Mr. Mason would discover the substituted camera, and, every time I imagined him suspiciously peering at a scratch that seemed too long or coming across a record of the Yashica's serial number, I studied even harder and vowed to be even nicer to my mother and my sister and especially to my brother. That was my bargain, the bargain I forged that summer night. Forged with whom, I'm not sure. But, in truth, it matters less with whom or with what we strike our bargains than that we keep our bargains, and I did. That was the year of Sputnik and Alaska statehood and the first nuclear submarine under the North Pole, and news of all those wonderful and forbidding things reaching little Ganaego also spurred me. I did not get *A*'s on every paper, nor on every exam, and occasionally my brother and I still fell into bitter rows, but most of the time I got good grades and most of the time my brother and I remained faithful friends. When I graduated from Ganaego High, my father and I didn't hug, as some fathers and sons did, but shook hands. And when I graduated from Case Western Reserve with a degree in mechanical engineering, my parents made the long trip to Cleveland on the bus. We never talked about any bargain I might have made. Indeed, Mr. Mason's original camera was put away and no one, in my memory, ever again referred to it. But I think my father understood my bargain. When I was to graduate from the University of Michigan with a master's degree, he suffered the first of his premature—and ultimately fatal—heart attacks, and my mother sent me a card with a formal apology and a small check.

I work for an aerospace firm in California. I work long hours, we all do nowadays. I am also married and have two children, and so, between work and family, I have little time for reverie. But sometimes I think of Ganaego and of the men who worked in the mill. On paydays, our very own cake-eater, who had come, for whatever reason, to live among us Eastern Europeans, Mr. William J. Pennystone, would drink a little too much. One night, Mr. Pennystone fell headfirst over the fence and slept in the small yard before the row houses, dreaming peacefully in a confused jumble of limbs until morning. A few years after my father died, the steelworks was shut down. The blast furnaces were toppled and chewed by a machine into bits and pieces, the coke ovens and office buildings were razed, and the nine-mile property along the river was graded by bulldozers and covered in dazzling white slag. People still live in Ganaego, people still like their town. But the whistle no longer sounds and the men no longer stream from the housing plans down the brick streets and through the main gate. All that, all that ended.

The Widow and the Scrivener

To Pernelle and Nicholas Flamel

Whether or not you and your hubby
unraveled the secrets of the universe,
or were visited by celestial day-trippers -
these assertions are irrelevant.
The fact remains: there was love,
and it was real, in spite of
your widow's weeds and the bowed set
of his scrivener's shoulders.

There was love, the deep and lasting kind
whose fire still burns after trysts among
dusty book stacks, and the bloom fades
from withered cheeks. And this is
what history can't - and won't - forgive;
the alchemical success of romance,
a capital crime committed by you both
against the miserable naysayers
who were never be able to match you.

A Guide on Loving Him

One night a woman is in bed with the man she loves and he has his back turned to her. He is sleeping, but she is not, and she thinks about the fact that recently she has seen little besides the back of her lover. She has memorized all the moles on his back (two next to his spine on the left side of his middle back, one off by itself closer to the lower back on the far right, and another one even further down, right above where the sheets cover him). She makes a constellation of these imperfections as she stares. It is a strong back, but pale from working inside. He doesn't lift many things, but he does yoga and she can see the long, flexible muscles even in his relaxed state.

He turns from her more and more every day. During the day it feels like a giving up, as he places his back to her while he cooks dinner, rather than look at her as she tells him about her day. At night it feels like pure exhaustion as he sighs and rolls over to his side. Sometimes she thinks it is just habit, unintentional in the pain it causes her to see him always facing the opposite wall. But if she kisses the side of his neck he shifts further away to let her know, as subtly as possible, that he just isn't in the mood. He gives almost no explanation—*I've been through so much. I can't handle it. I'm not sure about what any of it means any more* he says. She knows it's all bullshit, but he doesn't and the more he believes the bullshit the more of his back she sees.

At night, after he has fallen asleep and is gently snoring, she brushes his shoulder blades with her finger. Of course, she has had plenty of time to study his shoulders, but sometimes she doesn't even mind this because she loves them so much. She likes that they aren't too broad. Some of the men she's been with had shoulders that stretched on for miles. They seemed to want to take up an entire room—they demanded attention from her and other women, too (how could she forget all the other women?). She could never hold those men, her arms didn't fit comfortably around them in order to connect her hands at their chests. But not with this man, the man she loves. She could hold each of the protruding disks in the palm of her hand, if she wanted to. She could enclose him in her arms and squeeze him until he couldn't breathe, if she wanted to. If she wanted to. But she likes better to trace the shape of his shoulders with her finger and then sweep giant figure eights across his back. If he wakes up from this he never lets on. He just breathes. She sees his back expand slowly and contract again, but otherwise he does not move. It is hypnotizing to watch and feel his breath at the same time, but it only makes her joints hurt with a need to cover more of his surface with her body.

Some nights, she is able to find her own pleasure in the pain of her longing and this action of sweeping his back will lull her to sleep. But tonight she notices something. A tiny indent off to the side of his spine—slightly bigger than a fingernail imprint. Her nails are long (she hasn't bitten them off recently) so she pushes into the indent with her index nail. It slides in smoothly and she wiggles it around. It is warm inside her lover, tight around her finger which now feels as if it has grown twice its size while inside him. She sees the skin moving from the outside as her finger dances along the inside of the man she loves. She finds space for a nail from her other hand and she begins to pull apart her lover's back. The hole opens slowly, making no noise, as if it were designed to be opened in this way. When the hole is the size of a quarter she can see inside him. It is dark, mostly, but she sees the long, stringy sinews along the sides and can imagine further inside, the maze of bones and fleshy organs that make up her lover. She is pulling wider and digging deeper past the muscle until there is enough space to climb inside. Her lover does not stir as she crawls in next to his spine.

Place Names and Coverings

Calcutta: orange moon and midnight blue,
a glamor spun from ordinary charcoal,
from raw silk and soot, from sapphire
and mustard seed, pressed by hand
into a sacred fabric that clothes the self
and leaves the body naked.

Cypress: gust of scorched sand,
drawn through a needle so fine
it torches the air, fire eating filament
devouring bare shoulders,
covering the face, hands, feet
with thumbprints so bright,
they touch, they scald, they ignite.

Alma-Ata: green grass and gold tinsel
knotted on the fringe, a meadow
of threads with breezes through,
tiny movements catch at mirrors,
tin snipped and sewn onto the wind,
birds darting back and forth,
their songs and wings.

Peru: a pure llama wool that rests
on your arm like a patch of sky,
made strand by strand from yarn
on a wooden loom, braided with silver
ribbons, a blanket of blue lapis,
blue azure, blue anguish.

Acrra: colors glossy as the wings
of beetles—green, black, white—
made from emerald, ebony, and bones,
the cloth of survival, of renewal,
of ancestors digging in the earth,
repeating the pattern of daily ritual
and necessary patience,
a geometry plied
by women, for women.

Kathmandu: a shrine cloth stitched
on terraces of rice paper, prayer flags
hoisted to heaven's feet,
trampled under, littered with condors
and multicolored kites fastened
with bits and pieces of string.
Wherever you look the fabric is torn,
half blessing, half violation.

New Orleans: delta, silt, and spice
woven through the French Quarter,
tangled on a wrought iron loom
from balcony to balcony,
overlooking the strapless shoulder
of the Mississippi.
From the opposite bank of the river
nobody recognizes you
and the mud breathes like a crocodile.

New York: a covering made like a grid,
stone, steel, and glass, crushed
in a synthetic rash.
The loom this time is a scaffold.
There is bedrock and a beauty mark.

Vincent Barry

A Lot Like Limbo

"The unconscious can snuff out a meaningless existence with surprising swiftness. . . ." Jung said that. I read it in therapy. My wife insisted I go after she caught me in the kitchen in a torrent of sobs, and I blurted out everything about the girl.

A girl I knew a long time ago has come back, is what I said, just like that—both the girl and the way I said it, and a lot more.

I didn't mean physically—for all I knew the girl was dead, in which case I just knew I'd have to go back and throw myself on her grave—which I also told my wife. . . . I meant in memory—but just as real. She'd returned two days earlier, the girl had.

~~~

I had been idling at the computer at the time, scanning the online news when bango! a headline caught my eye. It was about a shooting, of a cop. That wasn't what grabbed me, though. It was the dateline. "Lakewood, NJ." The word froze me—"Lakewood." I mean it shut every thought out of my mind and—well, it held me is what it did . . . tight, like it would never let go. And I just sat there. . . . I don't know for how long— just staring at the word . . . spellbound.

I'd met the girl there, you see—at a dance. She went to college in Lakewood. But I wasn't thinking of that at the time—I mean I wasn't conscious of it, of her or the dance or anything like that—not when my fingers, as if attached to a hand possessed, typed L-A-K-E-W-O-O-D. And even afterward, after the word appeared in the search box, I just sat there— "unhurried, unflurried, unworried," as James once wrote of a character. . . . Funny, but I've been reading a lot of ole Henry since the girl came back. I don't know why. You know, "The Beast in the Jungle," "The Bench of Desolation"— anyway, where was I? Oh yes, sitting there, yes, I was sitting there, just gazing at the word . . . listening to its call . . . captivated by the inchoate allure of the beguiling word.

Bewitched, if you don't mind an old-fashioned word. . . .Well, old-fashioned to me. Perhaps because I always associate it with that old song "Bewitched, Bothered, and Bewildered."

I hardly know how to put what happened next. . . . I guess you could say I felt a stirred and curious desire . . . just to be with it—the word. . . . Like—what? Well, have you ever wanted to be with a love letter after you've read it? Just hold it? Maybe carry it around with you? Take it out every so often . . . touch it, feel it, even inhale it? Like that.

So, that's what I did—just sat there with the word, like a letter spread clear and bright before me. . . .Where's the harm?

The vague, evocative twinge of sentiment—well, that should have told me something . . . and, too, the subtle ache that went straight to the heart. But by then, I suppose, it was too late. By then the word had worked its magic, so to speak. It was—calling me, you could say . . . yes, summoning me. Where, why—I didn't know, only that I had to follow, unmindful of the clouding of disaster—the unheralded storm up ahead. . . . Looking back, it all seems so unwise—reckless even, like meddling with fate. . . . Oh sure, I'd read of the ensorcelling Siren song, but reading is one thing, recognizing another—if you know what I mean.

Anyway, with—with a kind of fierce urgency, I tried forcing my memory back, back, back to Lakewood. . . . And as I did I had the sensation of being in a heart-thumping race . . . of frantically pursuing a quarry as elusive as a ghost . . . of desperately needing to catch it, or at least get close enough to touch it—or die. Damndest thing. And get this—the faster I ran, the farther I reached out, the more it receded before me until— breathless I broke off the chase.

And there it all might have rested had I not stopped straining and backed off, unbent. And when I did—well, the memory—of the girl, I mean—it came forth like . . . like an apparition . . . like a contact with the beyond. . . . There was no turning back then—I can see that now. . . ."Lakewood," my madeleine—the word, her presence—they were about to ferry me back to a far away place a long time ago. A twilight zone between time and memory. . . a place I'd say a lot like Limbo—or what I know of it from the nuns and the Baltimore Catechism. You know, the place where the unbaptized dead go? Or used to before the church put that tenet to rest. I wonder where they go now, the unbaptized dead.

At any rate, a sudden rush of adrenaline—not at all unpleasant—then sent my fingers flying over the keyboard searching for the girl. . . . Harmless, ho-hum stuff to begin—town and gown trivia . . . address, phone number, marital status, that sort of thing. . . . An idle pastime—a frisson of excitement for a day that up till then had been, like most, unfolding without promise or threat, one of those undistinguished afternoons that pass unnoticed and fade like shadows into forgetfulness. Where's the harm?

I think it was when my head began to swim that I decided to write it all down. Or maybe the other way around. No matter, my head began to swim with a riotous swirl of images, coruscating with faces and old passions, and I felt an irrepressible urge to transcribe what I was seeing, hearing . . . but mostly feeling. Write it all down like—like, well, a letter—a love letter, really. Schmaltzy stuff like—

There's the dance floor where you first come in sight, a phantom of delight. A dancing shape, with smile so winsome and cheek so soft, an image to haunt and startle.

Like I said, schmaltzy.

~~~

As I wrote I listened to romantic ballads— over and over again, often the same one, mostly from the 30s, 40's, or 50s. Not that I knew the girl then, but because, as I said, I'm old fashioned. . . . I just let them seep into the letter, the old songs— "The Way You Look Tonight," "For All We Know," "I Never Knew What Time It Was," and such. Where was the harm in that?—in luxuriating in a burst of recovered youthful romance? in "steeping my thirsty soul in the reviving wine of the past"?

You catch my eye, and my heart stands still, the way you look tonight. Your girlish laughter, your sweet conversation, you make me dream by the look in your eyes. You smile, and I'm smitten; you laugh, and I'm flung into new possibilities. . .

. And all the way home you're there with me still, your tenderness calming my fears in the night.

Like that. Where's the harm—

~~~

I thought maybe I'd send the letter to the girl when I'd finished, and tell her—what? how I needed to hear from her, perhaps how—*once again I want to feel that old yearning, the exquisite thrill of anticipation, and, too, the bittersweet pang when no letter is left. The thrum of my heartbeat—waiting, waiting, waiting—just to hear from you, just a word to get me through. Oh, how slow the moments go between your letters. Reading the last, over and over again, holding it, tight and close; carrying it everywhere, guarding it like an amulet till the next arrives, then bundling it with the others, gently, lovingly, almost sacramentally, to cherish and savor, perhaps to warm me someday with their glow, when the world's gone cold and I'm awfully low.*

And suddenly—damndest thing—suddenly I wanted them, I craved them—how foolish after all that time!—but I needed her letters near to me, they were dear to me. . . . Then my breath caught in my chest and presto! they were there with me—all the stumbling words that told what our hearts felt—didn't they?—they were near to me, dear to me . . . and the way she looked tonight.

Well, it was all too much—I can see that now—too rich a mixture, the exquisite intensity of simplicity and tenderness. I should have pulled back is the thing . . . eased off . . . decelerated before I spun out of control. But, frankly, I couldn't. Didn't want to, I guess. The high-octane rush of memories was too powerful, too intoxicating. I was along for the ride now. To the street where she lived, to her house in Clifton, its row of rooms—*the living room, my favorite room, the room where we curl up after a Hurricane Saturday night. . . .*

The Hurricane in Little Falls—*with its corny tropical storm effect and cheesy boys band—but for all of that, for all its corn and cheese, my all-time favorite place, because I could feel in the night the nearness of you gliding over the floor. . . . And afterward—in the wee small hours of the morning, on the sidewalk, outside your house, where the street is empty and damp and your breath is like summer, and the traffic signal is blinking, the one down by the post office . . . and I can't bear to part till the very last minute, when in the hush of the night I hold out my hand, and my heart I see in it. "See you tomorrow," you whisper, and give me a tap of a kiss . . . and I'm counting again the hours till then—to midday Sunday dinner.*

~~~

That night I didn't sleep; couldn't, haunted as I was by the afternoon's dizzying events—hallucinations, if you prefer, but I don't like the word. It—what? Well, it robs life of its the romance, don't you think? At any rate, my mind kept revisiting the afternoon's landscape, that's the thing—unmasking more texture and nuance, spontaneously interspersing fresh retrospections—that sort of thing. And all the while I'm thinking, How can I be so along in years, yet young not so long ago?

Funny, but now the memories no longer brought nostalgia's sweet embrace. The soft, mellow light which in mid-afternoon had left me flushed with a warm wistfulness had already begun to fade in the pink and golden, then perse crepuscular rays of dusk. And as night deepened with indecent haste, sweet nostalgia grudgingly gave way to a gathering gloom . . . then to blundering and writhing thoughts, a delirium of disorder, a dark chthonic world of tangled emotions which climaxed in a nocturnal phantasmagoria that left me a not-quite-sane soul fighting chimeras and breathing fast. . . . And pacing—oh, the pacing in the night . . . all the while on the qui vive for—for what? Some fiery-eyed beast slouching in the dark, stalking the bedroom ready to pounce. And when it did—and did it!— it landed hard, gripping me in a panic fear, my heart thumping like a trip hammer, my eyes blind with tears. . . . Damndest thing.

The next day and the one after brought no surcease, only more tears like hard rain. When I tried to sleep, anguish shook my dreams and vexed me to wake. In one dream I saw a solitary girl in a blue jumper, perhaps eight or nine, with eyes like buttons and an aureole of hair, skipping rope—in front of the girl's house. In another, a man in black— just his bent, quaking back. He turned his head, to the left, away from an open grave, but not enough to show his face; yet somehow I knew, as you know such things in dreams, that he was

37

grieving the death of his wife. The happy girl, the sad man—the same effect. They woke me up crying. Mourning tears—no one had to tell me that. . . .

You have to see someone, my wife said when I told her all of this, and more, a lot more, of my immedicable griefs. Things that backed her up and buckled her knees—knotted her brow . . . tightened her jaws . . . put a look of torturing wonder on her face. Things that left her stunned, silent, shaking her head from side to side, working her lips under frightened eyes, swaying, leaning into the kitchen sink, all the color fled from her cheeks. Mine were flushed, with big hot tears coursing down them. And my eye lids felt puffy, the rims too, and my lips were trembling, and she kept repeating mantra-like, my wife did, in a tiny, quavering voice, You have to see someone, you have to see someone, you have to see someone—like that. . . . Who was I to object?

~~~

My therapist, a Jungian, said my problem was religious in nature. "Your picture of God," she said, "of immortality?—It's withered." Her tone wasn't pejorative. Simply matter of fact . . . like a gardener might say about a sick plant. "Your bleeding heart? It's distressed." Like that.

She recommended going back to the church, for proper care and management, I surmised, for the care of my soul—"if you're in good standing," she added. "Jung said—"

"And if I'm not?" I said.

"If not, it'll take longer," she said.

"Longer?" I said. Then, patience not being a virtue of a desperate man, "How much longer?"

She considered that a bit before saying, "How long does it take to journey through the solitude of a land that is not created?" Jung said that also, but I didn't know it at the time.

Going back to the church seemed faster.

~~~

The only Masses I'd ever known—and that was a lifetime ago, when I was an altar boy—were in Latin. I didn't even know if they said them

38

anymore, Latin masses. They do, I discovered, at least at St. Malachy's, every morning at 6:30.

I'm not an early riser; but since, you know, my crackup—well, let's just say the nights aren't sent for slumber. I've been getting up early—sometimes three, four in the morning. I walk the beach boulevard. There's a green light at the end of the pier that reminds me of Daisy's. After about an hour or two, when I'm near exhausted and have brought my tautened nerves to heel, I head home and try to sleep. But I always wake with a start. Anyway, I figured it was the least I could do to steady my hand, restore my psychic metabolism, so to speak—going back to the church, I mean. Besides, coincidence was involved, perhaps meaningful coincidence—what Jung called synchronicity. That's something else I learned about later.

You see, in a way I owe my existence to another St. Malachy's, at least from all I'd pieced together from Scanlon, the eponymous owner of my father's favored tavern.

~~~

My father's name was Patrick, but he went by Paddy or Paddy Mac—for McKenna. He had emigrated from Ireland in the infamous year of 1929. Not that a great depression could daunt a young Irishman whose own father had survived to tell about *an Gorta mor*. And he did, too—tell about the Great Hunger. *Why the potato famine*—that was his favorite descant—why it had happened. Well into his sixties when my father was born, the old tiller never tired of attributing Ireland's starvation to divine wrath cast upon the sins of the people—perforce taking umbrage with those "social reformer-Huns" across the Irish Sea who also saw the famine as a divine intervention, but to halt the Isle's deluded, fetishistic dependence on the humble murphy. Hmm, Catholics and Protestants—what can you say? The dispute, which my father recounted as tirelessly as his own had, interested me less than the fact that both parties claimed to know the mind of God. I envied them. I never have. . . . Well, maybe I did, or thought so—once upon a time. (That's another song I listened to a lot when I was composing my billet-doux—"Once Upon a Time.")

At any rate, all my father had to do upon arriving in his new land was to find a job, a better fate by far than having to "sit on a fence"— his father's oft-cited words of a pensive priest—"wringing your hands and weeping bitterly a destruction that left you foodless." Indeed— especially since the City of New York provided a stout young Irishman like Paddy Mac immediate prospects just behind the cast-iron facade of the Baumann Brothers Furniture and Carpets Store on East 14th Street. For therein was housed, in the store's upper stories, the Delehenty Institute, proving ground for future officers of the New York City Police Department.

Straightaway Paddy found himself securing the streets of Manhattan largely, he fantasized in his Celtic sentimentality, for the well-being of the girl he'd abandoned an Irish seminary for almost as soon as he'd clapped eyes upon her. He thought he'd won her, too, the girl, on the crossing over, somewhere in the sea of mystery, sometime between the second and third days out of Cobh. Alas, destiny demurred—doesn't she always? It turned out that Paddy's princesse lointaine had her smiling Irish eyes set upon a "top- drawer Yank," as she termed the gamin she vouchsafed to wed.

"And how did he come by—

"Dis blunt, brute fact?" Scanlon said with a brogue over a jug at one of our colloquies, long after my father's death. I nodded. "De 'ard way," he said, running a dimpled hand through his fierce, fuzzy red hair, "a way dat's bound to 'aunt a man's very soul." Shrewd green eyes beneath fat lids and a spurt of red brows shot an interpretive glance my way, and the heavy-cheeked, Bardolphian barkeep gave a short cough.

He asked me, Scanlon did, to picture the beatcop, a year or two on the force, directing traffic on the corner of 34th Street, right in front of Macy's. I did.

"Sure then, there Paddy stood when, as if 'twas written in de stars"— he made a vast circular gesture—"one of de bloody Parmelee company's wall-to-wall taxis, app'inted wouldn't ye nu wid both overworked brakes and driver, spun our bebuttoned member of New York's Finest ter de pavement."

I didn't need to picture my father, mouth dumbly agape, bracing himself on one elbow and shading his eyes with the palm of his hand— Scanlon demonstrated on the bar top. Propped up so, Paddy then beheld, "as if tru a Celtic mist, dressed al' in white wid 'an' ter mout'"— I imagined Jane Greer in *Out of the Past*—none other than his enamorata. A breathtaking turn of events that doubtless would have eased the blow of the erant cab had it not been—well, Scanlon provided the coup de grâce.

"Wouldn't ye nu," he said, "but de doxy wus den promptly whisked away from de ugly scene by 'er b'yfriend an' 'scarted back ter de cab"—then, leaning across the bar, in a conspiratorial whisper— "in whose back sate de young lovers were nestled scant moments before."

"Well," Scanlon went on, clicking his tongue and shaking his head, "'twas loike Paddy'd been clipped by de Brown Bomber . . . or de backswing of de Iron 'orse—'twas." The tapster's way of saying that Paddy's life had changed in a breath. On the instant he grew hard and bitter, then depressed in the vein.

For weeks, months even, he lived in a deep gloom, Paddy did, his room a roaring loneliness of loss and despair. He had lost his job— forced to retire on disability— as well as his girl. Their passing in a flash snufffed out of his life all color and beauty, leaving him locked in a dark cell of arrant despair. In time his lost love assumed epic proportions —"the first cause of his death, the first of his sorrow."

"Trut' be towl," Scanlon said, "'e seriously contemplated a return to Éire, Paddy did."

What he would do on the island of destiny Paddy didn't know, though Scanlon thought the holy priesthood loomed large when, on his way to the steamship offices—"te buk passage, don't ye see, on de sleek motor ship *Georgic"*—Paddy paused to seek in a church—

What it was he sought inside Paddy probably couldn't have said. But Scanlon knew what he found by chance therein, in a back bench reciting the noon Angelus: A spindly cousin, it was, with jug-like ears and severe crowding of teeth, who was all too cloyingly eager to lend a fishy hand to a troubled kin.

"'Ye 'av to meet Mamie Fahey—ye simply 'av to!'" is what Paddy said the cousin said, Scanlon said, embellishing: "De cousin's exact words dey were, spoken, don't ye nu, wid a falsetto v'ice dat wud brook no debate."

The breathy words, he went on, were reply to the star-crossed tale that'd poured out of Paddy "loike tears from a baby." And with those tear drenched words, which flowed directly in front of the offices of the White Star Line at 1 Broadway, to where the pair had shambled after leaving St. Malachy's, "de troublin' of der lives began." He meant Paddy and Mamie, their lives . . . and mine too, you could say. I was born about a year later, on the day the *Georgic* sank.

Given his riven heart Paddy wasn't exactly smittten with Mamie. Or as Scanlon aphorized, "'e di'n't get waaat 'e loiked, and di'n't loike waaat 'e got," adding, "sure, a class brew, dat." Indeed. But Paddy did welcome the distraction and in short order, and very much on the rebound, accepted the hymeneal yoke—"'e in black broadcloth, she in cream lace. "

Paddy'd bolt to Scanlon's after, or more accurately during, one of the ongoing skirmishes they waged, mère and père, with money, or the lack thereof, the tripwire. There was, in a word, never enough, an indictment that my mother lamented the last of every month, when the chipped, porcelain sugar bowl that held the monthly household allowance on the first unfailingly was bare as a bone.

"'Oi'm fed up wid livin' on quare street!'"

Ah, the remembered line—I could hear my mother tossing it like a grenade—that had sent Paddy running for cover to Scanlon's, "where 'e commenced to ply 'imself wid a b'ilermaker or two before tapering off to a night of jars."

Nigh the bewitching hour, Paddy, properly pollaxed, shuffled out to his '46 Plymouth, "which 'e never parked but down by de canal"— the barkeep lowered his voice confidentially and massaged the red sausage rolls at the back of his neck when he added, "to 'ide it from prying eyes, doncha ye nu."

Sometime afterward, "for an unknown reason," read the official police report, "the subject bolted like a shot through a narrow gap between a block wall and the solid concrete lip of a canal culvert, crashed through a chain-link fence and flew into the canal." The report noted further that a heavy flow of water rushed the 2-door sedan down the waterway under Bloomfield Ave., past the new A & P, right through the "dead-man" cable which was designed to preclude just such a fatal outcome.

"Oi know whaaat dat's loike," Scanlon said, this time to a bunch of the boys having a few lillys, me among them. "Oi meself nearly met me maker de seem way."

He hunched over the bar, Scanlon did, like a quarterback calling a play. "Oh, 'twas one gauzy night, 'twas," he said to the rapt huddle. "In a terrible ball Oi wandered into de parkin' lot an', wouldn't ye nu, Oi failed to stop at me own Studebaker. Sure den, didn't Oi meself shtumble into de slough"—chuckling—"all de while singing 'De Connemara Cradle Song'. . . ." Then, straightening up and toweling a mug, "An' drowned, too, Oi'd 'av, as full as a bingo bus on a Friday evenin' as Oi wus."

"And what saved you now, Scanny?" one of the boys said.

"Oi'll tell ye waaat saved me. Sure, 'twas a desperate, last minute lurch at de dead-man cable, dat's what." He bowed his head and molded his hands, then muttered, "T-G," for "thank God," to which the boys responded antiphonally, "Aye, T-G," but for one doubting Thomas, not me, who preferred, "Away on a that."

"Every word of it true!" Scanlon said, giving the narrowback the rough side of his tongue. Then, with hand upraised as if swearing an oath, "As Paddy 'imself 'd testify, kip 'is soul. . . . 'e was sleepin', don't ye see, in his old Delux—just nodded off, Oi guess—an' Oi scared the beejasus out of 'im Oi did when Oi tapped on 'is window lookin' every bit a drowned rat!"

"And then what?"

"'An' den waaat?' . . . Waaat do ye tink den waaat? Den oi went me way is waaat, an'—" his voice trailed off—"Oi guess Paddy ye cud say went 'is. . . . An' dat was waaat." His face contorted when he added, "Poor Paddy Mac." Then, shaking his head sadly, with a deprecating hand wave, "Pah, de felly shud 'av been priest."

"Aye" from the lads, in unison like a Greek chorus.

"An' failin' dat, not married," Scanlon said.

At least not like he did, I was thinking.

"Aye, dat's it," Scanlon said as if reading my mind, "not loike 'e did. . . ." Then, his eyes filling with pale distress, "Tis all ye really need to nu aboyt de felly, ain't it?. . . Oi mean to understand 'im an' all. Dat one t'ing, I mean dat 'e—

"It is . . . in a nutshell," someone said, "as they say."

"Aye, in de nutshell," Scanlon said, then musing, "Bad cess that," bad luck, then the breviloquent, "Der's no good outcome if ye don't catch dat line."

The lads at the bar were silent and cadaverous—me among them.

~~~

I took with me into St. Malachy's the image of Scanlon wiping down the bar counter, half meditating to himself, half to the assemblage, "Lacrimae rerum, lacrimae rerum."

~~~

The odor of lingering incense and the scent of oils—they were there. So were the white cross stoup of holy water and the stand of flickering red votive candles and the muted radiance of the stained glass windows and the antique wood reliefs of the Stations of the Cross. . . . It might have been a long time since I was in a church, but only if measured in years.

I half genuflected, gave a slovenly excuse for a signum crucis, and slid into a back pew on the gospel side, the "Mary side"—so named for her statue.

For Catholics the Mass is the re-presentation of the Crucifixion. It begins with the priest praying at the foot of the altar, symbolic of the cross, before ascending to the altar. But, funny, all I could see re-presented as the priest bent low, mumbling in Latin, all I could see—

get his—all I could see was my father hunched over our deep kitchen sink burbling something or other. Damndest thing.

I am close to him again—oh, I know I've slipped into the present, the present time I mean. But, you see, the thing is—well, I've been having a little difficulty lately with my tenses—I mean sorting them out—the past and the present, mostly. That's part of my problem, I guess. Not the future. That doesn't seem to bother me—not really. I don't think about it much, the future. Maybe because I've reached the September of my years, as the song goes, and the days are dwindling down to a precious few. . . . But the past—Jung was right, you know: The past is terribly real and present. Faulkner, too—"The past is never dead. It's not even past."

Anyway, I'm standing close enough to get splashed, as close to my father as the servers were to the celebrant. But, as I said, I can't understand him, my father, what with all his stertorous snorting. I see I'm holding out his favorite oversize white towel, the one he brought over with him, the one with the word KNOCK printed on it in bold dark blue—you know, the place of miracles? It's to be used, the KNOCK towel—and he's made this quite clear to me, mind you—it's to be used strictly for exorcising the "ferry dust," which is what he calls all the dirt and grime he draws like a magnet on his shift at the Hoboken ferry, where he worked after leaving the force—"ferry dust.". . . But, as I said, I can't make out what he's saying.

As the priest confessed his sins—*Confiteor Deo omnipotenti, I confess to almighty God*—I am suddenly, implausibly, madly reciting to myself, "A stoop-shouldered ferryman with gnarled hands knotted at the joints, scruffily attired in faded plum shirt and pants with frayed pockets, scuffed lace-up boots and floppy black cap with dull, cracked visor . . . whistle in right hand, receiving with left all manner of souls and their conveyances on and off the plucky *Elmira* for her ten-minute voyage across the great Muhheakantuck to lower Manhattan."

And as the priest ascended to the place of the unbloody sacrifice, I am adrift again on those placid crossings—gliding past the day's great ocean trundlers—the *Ilde de Fance* and *Mauritania* and, to be sure, the grand dames, *Elizabeth* and *Mary*, their whistles moaning mournfully—when my father, his eyes shut tight, reaches out and takes the towel from me and buries his jowly face in its flipside image—of the sky blue lady of said Knock.

Then he says, my father does, get this, Give us some music like a good fella, why don't you?

Ah! Of course, that's what he's been murmuring—my cue to crank up the Victrola for his favorite song. And he'll have none of the new Philco either or any of that John McCormack, no sir—not for his favorite song. Only the wind-up non-electronic 78-rpm gramophone will do for Franklyn Baur.

And don't let the breath out of it this time! he says, my father does, turning around abruptly to show again, and for as long as I live, the ever-present puzzle of gray-blue eyes with a weary yet restless look. Damndest thing.

I know the song by heart, like the Hail Mary, having played it for him so often. And once again I place the vinyl disc on the turntable, with the care of the priest setting the burse on the chalice.

Then my lips move quietly, prayerfully, with the first notes of the violinophone, shaping the words as I once could the *Suscipiat*, which I tried again, I did, honestly, after all the years, but stumbled beyond the first sentence— *Suscípiat Dóminus sacrifícium de mánibus tuis, May the Lord accept the sacrifice from our hands.* No matter, the words of the song are already crowding out the prayer. Those I recite flawlessly, as the priest prayed that our sacrifice might be acceptable to God the Father Almighty.

One little kiss, a moment of bliss, then hours of deep regret
One little smile, and after a while, a longing to forget
One little heartache left as a token
One little plaything carelessly broken

Remember the night, the night you said, "I love you"
Remember

Remember you vowed by all the stars above you
Remember

Remember we found a lonely spot
And after I learned to care a lot

You promised that you'd forget me not
But you forgot to remember

The song's last wistful refrain fades just as the server intoned the holy, holy, holy coming of Christ—*Sanctus, Sanctus, Sanctus*—and the ping, ping, ping of the server's bell broke my reverie. But not for long. For by the time the Anamnesis was done, the prayer of remembrance, my mind has slipped back and I am adrift again.

Why, why, why is "I Forgot To Remember" your favorite song? I ask my father, though knowing full well what he will say. I've asked him before, you see, many, many times, and he always goes, as now, suppressing a titter: I forget. That still makes me smile. But once—yes once, I recapture from one of memory's hiding places—once he broke our ritual.

It speaks to my soul, he said on that occasion, thickly, sadly.

I didn't fully understand, but I knew even then, as young as I was, it must be very serious if his soul was involved. That I remember.

Quare tristis es anima mea, et quare conturbas me? Why art thou so sad, my soul, and why art thou downcast?

What is this soul that the celebrant was calling sad and downcast and that my father's favorite song was speaking to?

"The soul is man's spirit, the part that will never die," so says the *Baltimore Catechism* and Sister . . . Sister . . . Sister what's-her-name.

Was that it, then? After all these years. Was that what "Remember" was speaking to—the part of him that would never die? Is that what he meant?

The priest was asking the Lord to be "mindful of those who have gone before us; and to deliver us from evil and, through the intercession of blessed and glorious Mary, ever a virgin, Mother of

47

God, peace in our days; and to find acceptable our lowly homage and sacrifice"—only in Latin.

And then he went, the father, *Ite, missa est—Go, the Mass has ended.*

Funny, but I had trouble— going, I mean.

My face was wet with salty, hot tears. That surprised me. I didn't think I could afford any longer "the cheering luxury of tears." But I could feel more brimming in me, and I rummaged around for something—a tissue, a handkerchief, anything. Finally, frantically, foolishly, I dabbed my eyes with the letter, the envelope that contained it, actually. Can you imagine?

That's when some lady asked me if I was all right. And that made me feel—strange . . . funny, but wonderfully strange. . . . Then the lady—I remember she had arrestingly liquid violet eyes—the lady said—she said something about remembering Mother Mary in times of trouble. Funny, but that made me feel stranger.

"And what did you say," the therapist said, "to the lady?"

" 'Let it be,' I said, 'let it be.' . . . Damndest thing."

The Well

In Waterford, Maine
I climbed down a well.
For a book,
To describe
The bottom of the well,
I climbed down,
As Bill,
The strapping rancher,
Bill:
Shoulders wide enough
To bear a multitude of sorrow.
With Bill,
I could climb down.
Deep down.
Terrified at first.
Terrified to look.
Terrified to step in.
But after 5 feet
I felt safe.
Cool, cold, chilled yet safe.
Flying spiders
And moss
And cobwebs
It all passed by me
Without fear.
The sturdy stones
Were a bold comfort
Like sipping a cup of tea
I leaned against the cozy rocks.

Cold chilling and warm

I go to a prison
Dark and wild
Murderous men
Hands and arms that slaughter.
But to my utter shock
An energy filters through
An energy pure and white and light and loving
Flushes through my veins
Cleaning
Burning out the hate
How?
How does descending to the abyss purify us?
How does the descent somehow uplift?

How?
Will the Angel of Death,
The Angel we dread
Also lift us up?
On his coal-black-fiery-wings
And carry us?
Carry us to a place of Burnt-away fear?
A place much less dreaded than we think?
Unimaginable now.
Unimaginable always.

At Farley's

William was the first to arrive. He rinsed his thermos in the sink behind the counter.

When Jon wanted to impress a woman, his conversation turned to the Golden Mean. He threw back his head to laugh and you could see the way coffee coated his tongue.

Ralph said he could talk to a banana peel but he preferred women. William took a sip from the espresso-sized thermos lid he held between his thumb and middle finger.

Nick grew a beard only on the right side of his face. His straw fedora drooped after a late night at the Boom Boom Room. He played blues piano but aspired to jazz.

"It's the way the Egyptians built the pyramids," Jon said. "The ratio of the longer side to the shorter side."

It was all very silly Karen believed, to think there could be romance at her age. But she could hope. She mentioned that Mary Ruefle wrote poetry by hand, didn't know how to type. Had a callus from gripping her pen.

The meter maid came round every Tuesday and Friday, ahead of the street sweeper, handing out parking tickets. The barista shouted a warning when she could. Jon yelled, "Fuck," mid-sentence, grabbed his keys off the table, and ran out the door.

Tom pulled out a Sharpie and drew a coffee cup on a page of the *Bay Guardian* and signed it so it would be worth a fortune after he died.

Curtis drew detailed plans for waste water systems in one of the journals kept on a shelf and instructions for making a paper butcher's hat.

There was a spot in the floor that squished underfoot from dry rot. We had an unquenchable thirst. We were in love with the Ducatis lined up outside at the curb. Someone complained when Annie the dog grabbed a scone off a plate and someone complained when the Health Department issued a fine. Mostly we laughed. We thought we had time.

When Jon returned, he picked up where he'd left off: "Of course, DaVinci was the master." No way he'd trust any gallery to represent him. That asshole Berggruen wouldn't even pop for decent wine at his opening in '93.

William screwed the lid on his thermos, folded the auto parts classifieds under his arm, and headed out in the 1965 white Volvo he called Pearl.

The Country of Marriage

The terminal was plush enough for the rituals of departure
but your train was late, delayed somewhere unnamed, so I
waited with you on Track Number 3, seated on
the grimy bench studded with cracked pink chewing gum,
some child's marker of territory or time

and wished you didn't hate airports or the destination or
whatever it really was that made us sit here, having said everything
that could be said, but still not enough, remembering taking the sleeper
from London to Edinburgh and diving underground just before arrival
in that chilly Scottish morning, crossing a border in our sleep

and the farmhouse where the family gave us tea and the daughter
slipped me a shilling to put in my shoe on our wedding day,
which, or course, I don't need now but keep anyway, like the smile
I create as your train pulls out, you, at a window, waving,
me, on the platform, wanting you to remember me, happy.

Armana

I live in a god's city, but apparently, it's the wrong god. Mother says its blasphemy to be here and that god lives in churches, but father says god lives wherever he damn well pleases and if mother hasn't actually met him, maybe his vacation home just happens to be the place we take care of. This place is Amarna, and it's falling apart. Down, rather. I guess apart makes it sound like it's coming undone but the stones still touch each other, just not the way they're supposed to. It's okay because it was built to look like this. I tell the tourists that the city is 3,346 years old but it's only eleven. Father built it the year I was born and when I tell the tourists that the city is on the bank of the Nile river, I have to ignore the BillyBurger sign that's eight feet taller than our wall and whisper to them that this year the advisor has predicted the river will rise more than normal and there's a chance the city might flood. They drink out of plastic water bottles and smile politely. They feel sorry for the boy who's also a tour guide and they know just as much as I do that the only river Amarna is near is I-37 and that the bellows of the hippos I point out are honking car horns. I don't blame them for not believing. God appears only at sunrise and we don't even open until ten.

Child protective services have been here again today but father explains to them that I'm not really working and it's family property and I volunteer. I nod say I want to do it because I really do. There are pictures of me on the living room wall and I'm a year older in each of them, dressed in a white linen kilt and smiling next to the sign that reads *Live the Past! Experience the home of Egypt's most infamous pharaoh, the heretic Akhenaton, here at AMARNA*. I only go into the details about how he wasn't *really* a heretic if someone is smart enough to know the history. There's one every few days or so and they think they're really smart and bring it up like I don't know, but I shoot them down like an

Ethiopian archer and say, in a voice that's too grown up for my skinny legs and lack of body hair, "People are often confused about the concept of advertising," and then they always ask how old I am.

I tell them I am twelve and a sophomore in high school and at first they think I am lying. But then when I explain that I am homeschooled they either nod, like it's a sad thing, or open their eyes wider, assuming I'm too smart for public school like their kids who complain about homework and demand cars when they turn sixteen. You know what I do for homework? Last week I made a pipe bomb that my mom actually helped me disassemble and then I wrote a short story about how a mathematics professor discovered that real analysis is a type of philosophy. Sometimes I think I'd like to be like other kids, putting wires into potatoes and making light bulbs glow, or getting dropped off at the movie theatre then giving parents angry looks when the parents don't drive off fast enough. But really, I like my life, and I love my parents. I tell them almost everything, but not how God comes to me every morning and tells me his secrets.

~~~

I get up at 5:30am and my physical education requirement is fulfilled by my morning run. I run three miles around Amarna, and when I'm done, I climb up the ramp into the ruins of the Small Aten Temple, flanked by columns made of mesh and fiberglass and constructed to look like stone, and I sit cross-legged facing East, waiting for Aten to appear. He rises over the complex wall, sometimes weak and diluted by clouds, sometimes strong and hot and violent. He speaks to me as the last of his body clears the horizon and everyday it's a small piece of knowledge, a koan for me to consider during the day. Sometimes I can't figure it out at all but sometimes I come up with an answer. My favorite days are the ones in which I come up with an answer but it *changes*. Those days I really think I'm learning something.

This morning I am thankful for the breeze because it's already in the eighties and as the sun comes up I hear his voice like water rushing out of the tap, and though it's fierce and quick, it pools in my mind where it becomes clear and still and I wait until the water is tired and the surface of the pool is at rest and it whispers again and again until I commit the koan to memory. Today I hear *when you can do nothing, what can you do?*

Like most days, I cannot comprehend what this could mean when I first hear it, but I repeat the phrase and whisper it to the wind and when I am sure I won't forget it, I walk back to our home in the King's House where inside instead of stone walls and dim, cloudy light, there is drywall and air-fresheners called "Island Breeze" in white outlets against sage walls that make our home smell too strong and the berber carpet is tan and stiff. Where my mother is making breakfast and my father is on the phone with Maribell, the woman who runs the concession stand in what's left of the coronation hall where we sell lunches with prices the tourists complain about. But they can't resist names like "Marinated Roasted Crocodile" (chicken), "Clay-baked Hippo" (pork), and the popular "Amarna Dog," which is the cheapest thing on the menu and is clearly just a hotdog. At least it's quality.

Dad is sitting with elbows on the kitchen table and one hand has the phone to his ear and the other is pressed over his eyes. *I know,* he says, *but maybe this isn't going to work.*

I know Maribell is strange. She's in her forties and her hair is pink, a color that dad has told her isn't authentic for the time, but Maribell won't dye it a natural color and I wonder if dad is finally going to let her go. Maribell is what dad calls an independent contractor and at night he stays up late and marks spreadsheets in red pen and he always has the checkbook out but never writes any checks.

Dad looks up and sees me and is saying *yeah, yeah, yeah,* and then he hangs up and without a word, leaves the room.

I sit across from where he was and mom puts a plate in front of me with a bagel and cream cheese and salmon and scrambled eggs and a bible.

"What's this for?" I ask her, fingering the crushed velvet cover with a name plate sewn onto the front. It's the book I see her reading every night in her bathrobe.

"It's a bible," she says, stating the obvious.

I fork eggs onto my bagel. I don't like to eat food separately. "But what's it *for?*"

"I think it's time we start doing things the right way around here." She's fingering the lace edge of her apron and trying to gauge my reaction.

"Did you know that Christ is a representation of Horus?" I ask her. "He's basically the same thing. I think the Christians copied the Egyptians."

She frowns hard at me.

"Solar deities are popular in all religions-"

"This place is poison," she says, and I'm surprised by how angry she sounds. I know mom would rather be in a regular house in the suburbs with a lawn to water and flowers to plant; dad won't let her have a garden here. He says it wouldn't be authentic. But she never tells *me* how much she doesn't like it. "Your new class is *Religious Studies* and we're starting with Christianity."

I am already doubtful that this class will study anything else, but this week we're going to make a solar panel and so I'm willing not to argue about this one thing. *When you can do nothing, what can you do?* I think about the question and decide that when I can do nothing, I will accept it and not complain. It seems like the right answer. An adult answer.

But it also annoys me. It's too easy.

While I eat, mom bangs the pan loudly in the sink and the front door closes. I open the bible blindly and read Proverbs 29:25: *The fear of man bringeth a snare, but whoso putteth trust in the Lord shall be safe.*

I don't want to make my mom angry by telling her that I don't believe in her god. I think learning more about Christianity might be a good thing. Any knowledge is productive.

I close the bible and see that I've left a white cream-cheese fingerprint on the aged velvet. I quickly rub it off but it leaves a milky smear. "We're out of toothpaste," I remind her, and she becomes very still.

Her back is to me and she says, "Today's history lesson is how the ancients used to make toothpaste."

"Does it work?" I ask.

"I don't know yet."

~~~

"You can see by these reliefs that the Egyptian canon of art was modified during Akhenaton's reign." I am showing a group of tourists the elongated bodies of the royal family with their hands outstretched towards the solar disk.

"They were aliens," a man says.

I turn towards him, still smiling. "It's true that the representations of the human form are altered," I explain, "but many experts believe that this was intentional and that Akhenaton wanted to distinguish his new way of life from the old by offering alternative depictions."

"Aliens built the pyramids too," he says, as if he's an Egyptologist and studied in Cairo.

I know his type. He is scared of foreign ideas and he's wearing a black shirt with a bald eagle clutching an American flag in its talons and his fanny pack is unzipped to reveal a crushed box of Marlboros.

"I'm not saying it was aliens," a woman next to him declares, "but it was aliens." She is smiling to herself and trying not to laugh and I smile wider at her. She's making fun of him and he doesn't understand what she's doing but he knows he's being challenged and frowns at her.

When you can do nothing, what can you do? Keep smiling and let the stupid be stupid, I think.

"We have a wonderful book on Amarna period art," I say to the crowd, eleven people, two families and two single adults. "Our souvenir shop has great resources if you're interested in continuing your learning experience at home."

The man's daughter has her arms crossed and I know they won't be buying any books.

"With that our tour is concluded," I pronounce. "Please visit our snack stand and enjoy the authentic taste ancient Egyptian cuisine."

The group doesn't ask any questions and they leave the temple through the front doors. Only one woman remains behind.

"Do you have any questions?" I ask her.

"Not really," she says. She is older, with dirty blonde hair put up in a bun and she doesn't look like a normal tourist. She is wearing a navy skirt suit and her pink lipstick clashes. We stand there and I am waiting for her to leave so I can go get lunch too. It's noon and I'm hungry.

"How old are you?" she asks.

"Twelve."

"And you work here?"

"Sure. My parents own Amarna."

"Don't you go to school?"

"I'm home schooled," I explain.

She nods. "Don't you ever want to go to a regular school? Hang out with kids your own age?"

"Not really," I admit.

"So you don't mind wearing that," she asks, referring to my costume.

"No. I'm told girls like a guy with a tan anyway."

She laughs and opens her purse. She pulls out her wallet.

"Please, ma'am, no tips. If you'd like you can make a donation in the souvenir store."

She takes two steps towards me and instead of handing me money she hands me a business card. "My name is Lisa Halpin. I've been assigned as your new case worker."

I don't understand for a minute, and then I realize what is going on. "You're with CPS?" I ask, taking the card and looking down at it. Her name is printed in boring black font and there's a phone number too. "I don't need a case worker," I tell her.

"I know you don't need one," she assures me, "but I'm here just in case."

"If you know I don't need one, then there's no reason for you to be here." I am twelve but I am not stupid.

"We're concerned about you," she says, as if the whole world has been watching me and is collectively concerned for my well-being.

"You should maybe talk to my parents," I say warily. I don't like being confronted this way and I feel like she's being sneaky.

"Yes, maybe I should. Can you tell me where I can find the office?"

I tell her where my dad is and she smiles. "If you need anything, you can call me any time."

"Okay," I say, but I know I won't.

Outside there are a few people milling about. I decide I don't want to eat at home and go to the snack stand to get an Amarna dog from Maribell. The man who believes in aliens is there with his wife and daughter and they're sitting on stone benches under one of the white canopies in the courtyard.

"Hi Maribell," I say, and she opens the metal cart with the steaming water. She knows what I like and there's already a bun in her hand.

"Hey Jacob," she says. I like the way she says my name. I don't know where she's from but she pronounces the second syllable like "cob," and I appreciate that because it's a short O, not a U, and people clearly don't study phonetics. "You talked to your dad today?" She puts the hotdog in the bun and then puts the whole thing in an oblong basket.

"No," I tell her, and pump three squirts from the ketchup into a paper cup.

"Oh." She seems disappointed.

"He should be in his office, but I think he's talking to someone right now." I don't tell Maribell about the woman. She looks like she wants to say something more, but doesn't.

"Not many people here today," I offer. The hotdog is wet and my bun is a little soggy.

"Not many people lately," she complains, and she's right. Seems like the last couple of years fewer and fewer people have been coming. "I think I'm going to have to get a different job."

"But you can't leave," I tell her. "What are the people going to eat?"

She points over the wall at BillyBurger. "Listen, Jacob. I'm going to leave," she admits. "I bought a food truck and already paid rent for a spot over at the university campus. I wanted to tell you myself. I'm just not making it here."

"Does dad know?"

"I'm going to tell him today," she admits. "But please let me do it, okay? I owe him that much."

"Yeah. Okay. You're still going to come by, though, right? And visit?"

She doesn't respond right away and I know she won't. "Hey Jacob, do you ever think it might be good to, you know, be in school? There aren't a lot of people for you to talk to here."

I look at her and I can tell by the way she's not really looking at me, but looking at the American alien family, that she's the one who's been calling CPS. I put the half-eaten hot dog on the cart between us.

"Thanks for lunch, Maribell. Maybe I'll see you sometime."

"Wait, Jacob."

But I'm already walking away.

~~~

From one to four I do school work. It depends on the day but today my mom has left a list of my lesson plans and says she's gone to do errands. I am supposed to read about gene mutation and 3-D geometry and then I'm supposed to work on my Shakespeare paper. We're reading *Hamlet* but I don't know why because *Hamlet* is so over-rated. I decide I don't want to write about *Hamlet* at all and instead of doing science and math I start to read *As You Like It*. Shakespeare's comedies were always my favorite.

When I am done with reading the first act I do an activity where I tape a congruent triangle over our globe and learn that the angles are all 90 degrees. The gene mutation chapter is kind of boring and I don't have any interest in bean pods. I read ahead and see that next week I'll get to learn about fruit flies and that I'll get to put them in the freezer to stun them and look at them under the microscope.

At five I am supposed to walk the complex, check the buildings to make sure there aren't any stragglers, and then I lock the gate. I keep my costume on while I do this. I don't want to ruin the authenticity of Amarna.

The food cart area is closed up and I see that Maribell has taken her Amarna dog cart and the chip display rack. I swing by the front office and see my dad inside on the phone. He is arguing with someone and so I grab the keys, wave at him, and make my rounds. At the end, I stop at the Small Aten Temple and think about my koan.

When you can do nothing, what can you do?

I don't what the answer is. Some days it's like this. I can come up an answer, but don't feel like it's *the* answer. I decide that maybe there isn't an answer, that the koan is circular and that maybe the answer is something like *when you can do nothing, you think about what you can't do, like answer a koan.*

When I get back to the king's palace at six there is no dinner but my mom is in the kitchen and she is sitting at the table with a suitcase on the floor beside her.

"What's up mom?" I ask her.

"We're going to gandpa's," she says.

"Why?"

She looks uncomfortable and shuffles her feet under the table. "Because it's not working here."

"What's not working?" I get a feeling in my stomach, like a hot walnut is in my gut and I refuse to step any farther into the room. My mom looks old and worn and for the first time I really see how tired she must be because she's not wearing any makeup and there are dark circles under her eyes.

"This. This," she says, gesturing to the room. "Everything."

"Yeah it is," I tell her. "It's great."

"No, it's not." She says this the way the man in the eagle shirt said that aliens built the pyramids. "Go change your clothes. We can talk about this in the car."

"No!" I say, and I realize she's gotten louder and I'm getting louder too. "I'm not leaving. Not without dad."

"We're leaving," she says and she stands up. "Go change your clothes."

"I'm not going," I yell.

"Stop being a child."

"I'm *not* a child," I yell. "I work and I go to school and I teach myself stuff and I'm smarter than you."

I said it. I said what I've been thinking for the past year and I can tell by the way her face is pale that she knows it's true.

"You know what?" she says, and she says it quietly. "You're not a child. And that's my fault. You talk to your dad tonight. If you're not a child you're old enough to know what's really going on. When you talk to him, you call me at gandpa's, and I'll come get you."

"Is this about the CPS lady?" I ask, and I'm almost crying now because I don't want mom to leave and I've just said something mean but I'm not going to take it back because I know I'm right.

"Partly." She picks up the suitcase. It's grey and purple flannel and I remember that the last time I saw it was when we went to Washington to see the museum complex. "Talk to your dad."

She is walking out and I yell at her, "We don't have any toothpaste!"

"We don't have any money for toothpaste," she says.

~~~

Hours later, dad doesn't come home and when I go to the office he is at his desk and papers are everywhere. I don't want to talk to him, yet, I decide.

I go to the closet where we keep our camping gear and pull out my sleeping bag. I get the pillow off my bed and don't feel like changing clothes.

On the way to the Small Aten Temple it is quiet and dark and the sky is clear. Last week I learned about different types of stars and even though I knew already that our sun is a star, I was kind of angry that it was lumped in with all the others. It's a special star. And not just because it's the closet one to our planet. It's special because god lives there and I know he does because he talks to me and gives me secrets to unravel and it's unfair that other people will not be able to acknowledge this.

The stars in the night sky look kind of puny. Twinkle is a stupid word and these stars do that stupid thing. They don't blaze and heat like the sun. Yeah, maybe somewhere in outer space they're boiling and exploding, but I can't tell that. I've seen pictures of the sun, solar flare magma arcing across the surface, and that is real and powerful.

I unroll my sleeping bag in the ruins and look up at the sky. I wait for the sun to come up.

~~~

I don't remember falling asleep but when I wake up I am stiff and my right shoulder hurts from where I've been laying on it. My shendyt is rolled up around my waist and no one's around to see my underwear, but for some reason, I'm embarrassed anyway. My dad has clearly been here. There's a water bottle and some cookies on the stone alter next to me. I don't know if they're for me or Aten.

I sit cross-legged on my sleeping bag as the sky lightens. I don't know if I should call my mom or not. I don't know if I should talk to my dad. I know I'll have to do both but I am waiting for Aten to speak to me first.

When the sun breaches the horizon I wait for the water words, but none come. The only think I hear is my own voice asking *when you can do nothing, what can you do*, and I think the answer is *wait*.

Polaroid Memories

Time doesn't
belong to the future,
where every day
holds onto the past.
Where it lives,
we are delivered.
We carry our minds
in buckets until
it pours into
a shadows past,
and if it's lost,
do we still
glance back
at old backs,
and recessed
memories?
Fabled melancholy
melodies that
mop our lives
still continue
to persist,
where harmony
refuses to age,
and if we still
peak at generations
of grandfathers
and cobwebbed clocks,
will we become
deceased declarations,

or successive
retaliations?
When time
is wound back
into the past,
tomorrow will
be yesterdays
repetition,
and like
a star gaze
in the
opaque night,
we hope that
we don't ever
lose sacred
sights.
Waves ascend,
then dissipate.
As dye fades,
our past
refuses to be
a placebo
when the
future is a fable
in a distant memory.

I'm Nothing Without You

Straight shot, microbolt. Sit up, sweaty sheets, vision blurred in shadow. Her face. I remember—skin loose beneath her eyes, sagging. Her cheeks rippling, flesh sloughing away, crimson drops splashing at her bare feet. Mouth opens, black gaps between the teeth that remain. Hair blowing out in clumps, northerly breeze, brushing across my face as it leaves her. Hot, wet fingers take my hand, stick to me as I pull back. No sound, silence in the dark, just the creak and groan of her body settling. Her eyes on me until they roll away, past my feet, into the gutter and down the storm drain. A scream, my scream, but not in this moment—in a future moment, echoing back through time and memory. Now, just this, only her. Only what is left.

Dr. James Crow

He sits us all down, piled on the bench, says
even if you love the unemployment,
even if you love the drugs, you have to turn
to the walls of health care, theirs, get caught up
in the courts; it's part of the slave-anthem,
the echoes of the future. Here is you—hopeful.
Here is you—fucked. The sky all filled
with God. Of course, it's not your sky.
Yours is filled with smoke. They call it
clouds. Don't let them fool you.

And So Go the Spoils

Victor frowned at the dimple of bellybutton in his stretched white undershirt, a case over an overstuffed pillow. The bottom seam hung away from the band of his boxer shorts. He tried to suck-in his pregnant gut, but that required muscles he'd long since lost to his office chair. Thirty years of sitting seems to make things spread. Turning to his side, he pulled his shoulders back and stood up straight. He still looked fat.

A girdle would help, but might be a bit awkward for the occasion. "Pretty hard to explain if I get lucky later," he said.

Fat chance.

"What happened to you?" he said. "Who are you?"

"I'm you at fifty," he reflected.

It couldn't be. His eyes weren't cracked at the corners with years of stress. He didn't have grey chest hair, or wrinkled knees.

"Oh, but you do. These are the lines of the days and hours and minutes of your life. You're wrinkled and grey because you spent your twenties mixing narcotics and alcohol like you required them to live."

Victor ran his hand across the soft mounds on his chest. Once two solid muscles he could make dance on command, now the only time they *didn't* move was when he was lying on his back. He squeezed one, a handful. "B Cup, Where is the body that once scaled a chain-link fence for a hot piece of ass? I was a god once."

"Not with this body, or this flaccid, sad looking cock. When *was* the last time you masturbated? Weeks? Months? Can you even get hard?"

Where there once was the heat of an active volcano, his sexual desire now burned more like hour-old coffee. He'd eyed the waitress at Bizztro where he and all the other business men ate lunch. Watched as she picked up a discarded napkin, her shirt opening just enough to see down into the dark of cleavage. Thought of her lips touching his. How her tongue might feel flicking back and forth on his old, used up dick. Just when he thought the smoldering coals of his libido would ignite – nothing. Then she'd move on to trick the *old* men into letting their wallets flow freely by leaning over to let them stare at her tits.

Really, the *old* men?

"Tonight is different."

"You think this forty-something you've never met will sleep with you?"

"Rita said we have a lot in common."

"Rita? The twenty-five year-old at the front desk? All she knows is that you're both old."

"And desperate?"

"It used to be easy. Can you even remember?" the reflection said.

He did remember. There was Charlotte, or was it Carla? They met his freshman year at one of his frat parties. His stature, on the social ladder and in height, towered those around him. Victor didn't hide that he knew.

Hendrix or Marley was playing. Or Zepplin. Sitting at a table in the kitchen, Victor was playing a game of quarters with one of the older brothers. Winning, of course. Harold Fretter was his best friend at the time, now, married with five or six kids and running a successful boat dealership in Florida. Fretter and some other douche were watching from the couch with two girls. One was Fretter's girlfriend of the month, Minnie. The other was Carla, Minnie's friend. Two weeks before she'd scratched her nails up Victor's thigh, but he'd already made a bet with another brother he could bang this Suzanne Somers look-alike. He'd even joked that Carla looked more like the other roommate from *Three's Company*, the one with boyish hair and a flat chest. He'd put Carla in his back pocket and won the bet.

While they watched Victor sink quarter after quarter, Fretter and the others passed a joint. The other guy was trying to make a move on Carla, but her gaze stayed on Victor. He winked at her, bounced another quarter on the table, and made his opponent drink a whole beer. Victor stood, hands in the air, and said, "Victorious."

"Yeah, yeah," Fretter said, clapping.

As though invited, Victor squeezed between the two girls, pushing the other guy into the arm of the couch.

"Dude," he said. "You mind?"

"Forgive my big dumb friend," Fretter said.

"I can speak for myself," Victor said, reaching for the half spent splif between Fetter's fingers. He took it and held the joint to Carla.

"My deepest apologies," he said. "Ladies first."

She pinched the joint from his fingers and put it to her lips. She took a long drag and her eyes, burning with the embers of spent weed, transfixed Victor. Removing the joint from her lips, she puckered and blew a thick cloud of smoke into his face. Without moving her body she passed the joint over his shoulder to Minnie and told Victor, "You're excused." He caught the scent of roses, and something more primal, like blood.

"Wanna see my room?" he asked, motioning with a nod of his head.

"Hey man," the guy said, "that's not cool."

Carla leaned in, her soft lips touching Victor's briefly. She said, "Lead the way."

At the mirror, Victor put his fingers to his lips. He'd been a jerk and Carla followed him to his room. When had he lost it? After the first accident?

"They started losing interest. Like word had spread."

One break-up after another without so much as the tip. Making him wait before they let him fuck them. Condoms helped, no more accidents. But dating wasn't working. Casual hook-ups were the way to go. But it was hard to go back to real relationships.

"The good ones said I was boring."

"And the bad ones?"

"Not mother material."

This blind date, it seemed like that one last ol'college try. Maybe she did want the same thing.

"Is that why you're going?"

"Maybe we'll hit it off. Maybe she wants kids."

"And that's it? Just hit it off to have kids?"

"I don't know anymore."

"Pussy."

Checking his watch, he found a pair of jeans on the floor near his bed and a wrinkled blue button-up shirt hanging in his closet. His iron had broken two years before, and cubicle life made it easy to justify wearing disheveled clothes. Back at the mirror he tucked and un-tucked his shirt, finally deciding un-tucked better hid his belly. He patted down the few strands of hair still clinging to his scalp before pulling his LSU hat backwards onto his head.

"You look like a jackass," he said, throwing the cap. He rushed out the door before the voice could follow.

On the way to the restaurant, his eyes kept retreating to the rearview mirror. Streetlamps were throwing flashes of light onto a woman in the car behind him. She wore little make-up. Her hair was in a ponytail. And there was a sweat stain in her spandex top between her tits. But Victor's attention was drawn to the two small heads moving in the backseat. At a red light, he watched as the two boys' faces appeared between the front seats. He wondered what their names were. They were laughing but the woman was facing out her window, fingers cradling her chin. Victor thought he could hear their laughter, and knew what had them so excited. He chuckled with them. Twisting, he looked in his own backseat.

The woman honked. Victor jerked and saw the light had turned green. "Stupid bitch," he said, as his car lurched forward. Victor twisted the radio's volume knob like he winding a clock.

In the parking lot of the restaurant, he stood and pulled his jeans up. His belt cut into the pudgy flesh near his bellybutton. "You're going to pop a blood vessel," he said.

Closing his car door, he noticed a young couple watching from across the lot.

"Stop talking to yourself," he said and turned towards the restaurant

Karen, his blind date, had already been seated and was working on a martini the consistency of swamp water. Maybe she'd be loose by the end of dinner. Then, they shook hands. Her grip matched his. Firm handshake equals ballbuster. But he sat at the table anyway.

Victor could see she'd been a hot piece, but she must have worshiped the sun. UV rays had roughed her up like an abusive luffa. At their postage-stamp-sized table, Victor hid behind the laminated menu. The restaurant was at capacity, the tables crowded with families and college students. A large group of coeds sat at the next table. Concealed by the large laminates, Victor scanned the row of perky tits like a cartographer studying a mountain range.

"Have you been here before?" Karen asked.

Victor said, "I'm sorry?"

Pulling the top of his menu down, she asked again, "Have you ever eaten here?"

Karen's tits weren't as interesting. They were more like his soft mounds than the girls' pointy Mt. Everests. "Yeah, all the time. And yourself?" he said and drummed his fingers on the edge of the table. His tongue burned for a scotch.

"I've come here with my girlfriends for drinks. This is my first time at a table," she said, sipping her dirty vodka. "I always thought this was a kid place, ya know?"

"No, it has a New York feel. Exposed brick. Naked rafters," Victor said. "The raised bar is all candles. We could move up there."

"Well, it just seems a bit of a college hangout." She laughed. A baby cried from across the restaurant. "That and families. All these damned kids."

What did that mean? She doesn't like kids?

Karen finished her drink and pinched the edge of the toothpick skewering two olives. She held the first between her red lips and slid it into to her mouth. They looked like testicles. Victor watched with interest until she crushed one between her teeth.

She held the other towards him. "Want one?"

"No thanks," he said. Ballbuster. "You're nice to offer."

She chewed the other one, and said, "Is Victor a family name?"

Victor wrinkled his nose at the sting of vodka and brine on her breath.

"No, I was named after some statue found in the Adriane Sea the year I was born."

"The Adriatic Sea?"

"Yeah, that one."

"I don't remember a Victor in Roman mythology. They just stole everything from the Greeks, anyway. Zeus became Jupiter, Zeus' son Hermes, the messenger, became Jupiter's son Mercury. Do you have much interest in mythology?"

"Not really," he said, and finished his drink. "I guess you know a lot from art classes?"

"I read a lot."

"I never read."

"Hmmp," Karen said. "Nothing, not even the paper?"

He'd learned not to follow this conversation, and definitely never say books are for nerds. But he was saved when the waitress brought his drink and took their orders. Victor gulped his scotch, and let Karen talk about her career at what she called "the firm" as though she were a lawyer. He kept comparing her tits to the girls' at the next table. They had smooth, happy valleys. Karen's tits just looked sad.

"I'm the best designer in the city but I still get shit jobs creating business cards," she said and laughed.

Victor finished his drink and ordered two more for the next round. The girls at the next table were growing louder, but Karen's drone was too powerful for him to catch their conversations.

There had to be something he could do to get their attention. His stomach gurgled, and he caught his reflection in the window over Karen's shoulder. Ol'college try? Kids?

"So, what have you designed?" he said, trying to feign interest.

"Have you seen the new exhibit at the museum?" she said.

Did he roll his eyes? He must have because Karen said, "Not a fan of museums either?"

"What, no I was trying to think of the new exhibit?" He couldn't recall even one. "Is it the Plato Exhibit?"

Karen jerked. "Yes, that's the one."

And that was a quarter splash. He could win this round. But did he really want to?

As she detailed her advertising campaign, he began chancing more glances at the girls. There was an empty seat at the center of their table. He would have squeezed in were he still in college. He saw himself sitting with them. His chair, like his purple and gold hat, was turned backwards. His arms folded over the back, he pulsed his biceps, testing the strength of his t-shirt. Every eye, ear, and nipple was focused on him as he told the story of his victory in the mud football tournament. The girl to his left whispered in his ear...

"Chicken fettuccini?"

His brain snapped like a rubber band.

"Sir, chicken fettuccini?"

The waitress held a bowl of noodles in front of him. Leaning back, Victor said, "Yeah, that's mine," and looked up at Karen. Her eyebrows and lips had twisted. He put his hand to his mouth and coughed. What was that, the reflection said, an apology?

"Can I get anything else for you folks?" the waitress asked, smiling at them.

"Yeah, two more please," Victor said. "Anything for you, Karen?"

"I'll have another martini," she said, returning the waitress's smile. "Thank you."

Victor unrolled his silverware and thought about tucking his napkin into his collar as a joke. Karen began eating. That she had ignored his daydream flipped his opinion of her ballbusting.

"How's your pasta?" he asked and smiled.

"It's good," she said, "better than the conversation."

"Sorry. I haven't been on a date in a while," Victor said.

"It's okay," Karen said. The waitress returned with their drinks and Victor swallowed one in a single gulp. Karen continued, "I have a tendency to prattle, I suppose."

"I'm not used to conversation. Well, not conversations with women. It's all numbers and football in my world," he said. And conversations about women, he thought. "Do you have any kids?"

Karen snorted. "No, I was never the nurturing type," she said, grabbing and swallowing half of her drink. "I can't have kids, anyway."

Victor's face grew hot and he felt the need to spit his food back into his plate.

"You can't?" he said. "Why not?"

"Do you have any children?"

"Almost," Victor said. His jaw loosened and he wanted to swallow back the word. It was too late. He could see Karen dissecting it.

She said, "What happened?"

He said, "I was young. Why can't you have kids?"

She said, "I was young. I'm too old now, anyway."

He said, "Too old?"

"Yes, don't you think you're too old to start a family?"

"I'm fifty, people…"

"That doesn't depress you?"

"What?"

"The thought of having a child, now," she said. "I mean how old would you be when they're twenty? If you're still alive."

Victor finished his fifth whiskey. His ears were ringing with the din of the restaurant, but Karen's last sentence echoed, taunted. He wanted to laugh at her. Push away from the table and join the girls next to them. Take off his shirt and swing it around like he used to at parties.

He said, "I'm not that old."

She laughed. "Well, I am. And those girls are too young."

Victor stood and dropped his napkin on the table.

"Excuse me, I need to take a piss." He raised his hands above his head, but dropped them quickly.

He weaved through the waiters and waitresses in the tight hallway leading to the restrooms. He latched the stall door and caught his weight with a hand on the red brick wall. It was gritty and cool against his palm.

"You're losing out there."

"I could still be a father," he said as he read the names and messages carved or written with black markers in the rectangular bricks: "Mark likes beer. – Jimmy's the Shit! – Slop Twat. – I got ass in here – Me too!"

Zipping his pants, he reached into his pocket and hooked his finger through his keychain. He flipped through and found the key he used the least. Leaning on his left forearm for support, he began to carve his name in a blank brick. His hands quivered, and the second line of his "V" slashed below the first. Red specks sputtered from under his key and hit his cheek.

Victor finished the "r" and stood back to see the wall as a whole. His resembled the writing of a boy first learning to write. He breathed in deep, the ammonia of old piss burned his nostrils.

"Good enough," he said as he left the restroom without washing his hands.

"Sorry, too many whiskeys, I guess," he said when he got back to the table.

"I asked for the checks," Karen said, nodding towards two black receipt books. "And some boxes."

Victor nodded, eyes on the table. The group of girls had left, their table sat empty, disheveled. He sucked back the last piece of ice in his glass.

"That's okay." He leaned back in his chair, propping his elbow on the back of the chair. He crunched ice with his mouth open, and said, "You're not my type."

"Thanks for dinner," Karen said, pushing both checkbooks towards him. She hooked her arm through her purse, stood, and walked away.

As she passed Victor on her way out he called, "What? I'm not good enough for you?"

Karen walked on, head down.

Victor paid the bill, and boxed both meals. "I paid for them, I'm going to eat'em," he mumbled.

He moved to the bar and ordered two more whiskeys. He'd won, right? "Made her look like a fool. No kids with that one."

Two girls, one blonde one brunette, from the table of coeds were sitting at the bar. Victor walked over and hovered between them.

"How are you ladies tonight?" he asked, doing his best to hold his shoulders back and suck in his gut.

"Super," the blonde said. "Looks like your date didn't go so great."

Victor swayed, put his arm on the back of her chair. "Yeah, she was an old hag."

"Aww, that's too bad." They both giggled, and the blonde slapped her friend on the knee.

His head felt like it was hovering above his shoulders. "But I was Victorious." He laughed. "My name's Victor. Get it?"

The girls didn't laugh.

"Can I buy you ladies a drink?"

"We're friends with the bar tender," the blonde said.

Victor saw his opportunity. He waved his hand and said, "Hey, buddy, service?"

"Be nice," the blonde said, rubbing her hand down Victor's arm.

"Excuse me, I'm a big dumb animal, sometimes," he said. He laughed alone. Then, he thought of Fretter and his family.

"Karen couldn't handle her drink like me."

"We only like top-shelf," the brunette said, winking at her friend.

"I only buy top-shelf," Victor said.

"Who's Karen," the brunette said, "your date?"

"Yeah," Victor said, trying to suppress a burp, "can you believe she doesn't like kids."

"Do you have kids?" the blonde asked.

"No," he said, "And, wouldn't want'em with that frigid bitch."

The bartender appeared. "She was pretty," the blonde said.

"Too bad," the brunette said, "guess you'll be going home alone."

"Maybe not," he said, moving his hand to the blonde's shoulder.

She shrugged, and the bartender glowered at Victor. "This *old* guy bothering you?"

The boy's eyes looked familiar. Victor saw the fallible assurance of youth, the glint he no longer saw in his own. He turned to the blonde. "Am I that old?"

"You could be my dad," she said, pity saturating her expression.

"Get the message?" the bartender said.

Victor looked over the bartender's shoulder to the mirror behind the bottles of liquor. He held the gaze of his reflection, no longer unrecognizable. He *could* be her dad; he could have been a father to any of them. He relaxed what little hold he had on his girth. Let his belt slide down.

He patted his stomach.

"You're right," he said, taking a sweeping glance at their chests, "you girls be safe."

He returned to his end of the bar, stumbling as he sat. The bartender followed, gave him a glass of water and said, "Didn't mean to spoil your fun, old man."

He watched the girls lean towards the bar tender, the blonde's hand on his arm. "Be careful with that one."

Victor sipped his water. It cooled the alcohol and embarrassment flaring in his stomach. But a desire still burned. One he doubted he'd ever be able to extinguish.

To Marlon Brando and All My Friends Lost in the Fray

Brando,
  my man,
     I am LOST!

I've put mucho faith in what I can't see
and have ended up with a pocket full of lint.

I over-hyper-drudge analyzed the scenes:
  the breakdown,
     which I'm pretty sure was scribbled by a secretary.
  The script,
     which I'm pretty sure was super-glued together.
  The soul,
     which . . . come back to me, I still haven't found it yet.

But Brando,
  Jim Carey asked me to "choose love"
    over "choosing fear."
      I'm afraid there's a "choosing too late."
        ~~~

Here at Loa,
  the mescal has too much pepper
  for what I have to offer.
  I've drowned in lemon bitters
  and American Spirits
  and I feel all my acts unraveling.
  I feel the bite take a piece of my heart
  in this path of love I chose to take.

With each sip
  I sense-memory her kiss on my lips,
  I feel her sweat on my fingertips.
  I lost track of time . . .

                    Is it June already?
                    ~~~

When my dog Rocko and I move out West,
  I'm hoping he'll still believe in me.
  I'm hoping he'll still believe
  I'm the only creature capable of spooning out the can food.
  He'll still believe in my ability to sustain him,
  in how only I can scratch that spot behind his ear
  which makes his leg twitch like Thumper's.
                    ~~~

The thought of suicide
  crossed my mind once like train tracks.

They're still there,
  grown mossy and covered with dry twigs and oxidized to
shades of green,

  but they're still there

(I choose truth above
  lovefeardeathjoy,
      Jim).
                    ~~~

It's too damn hot in here, Brando,
the glass and I perspire,

wishing both our faces are like the cool white marble
tabletops,
    not like the candles on the wall:
        shotgunned in no particular pattern.
        Light bulbs dangling above us in glass brains.

I grab the martini glass,
take another sip,
and stare at the blonde sitting on her lover's lap
as they share a bike taxi with black velvet seats.
    Their hands holding in soft peachness,
  her pink dress revealing tanned shave lines.

I hope she can't see my eyes staring through the window,
over the cocktail in my hands.
       ~~~

I still think of the love I lost:
  what she's wearing,
  how she tried and succeeded at looking cute
  in a flower top and plum skirt
  on our first/last "half" date.
  I grabbed her hand and she told me she was guarded
  and I trembled
  and stroked her knuckles against my cheek.

She giggled like bubbles,
  "you're cute when you wanna be."
  I also just really liked her touch.

Really.
      ~~~

Brando, my man,

the shortest distance between two points is a straight
line.
So where does that leave people like you and me?
Our entire existence is based on subtleties,
on how we filter the subconscious
through thin mesh wire strainers.
It pours like tequila and eggwhites and Basil Hayden
into the here and now.

It's just in our nature:
my ability to never let anyone go
will be my shiniest tool
and my dullest point.

Everyone leaves, my man,
I have to hold on while I can.

Leash Laws

I perch in trees, like a squirrel or woodpecker, always looking over people's heads, spotting a bald spot or the flat part where their hat rested too long, warming the owner's ears. It's not like I'm nimbler than the others, just keener in my vision.

No one knows when his or her tree-time will come. Some folks seem to be glued to the earth with sinews underground like electrical wires. They talk to each other in a way that wastes language, not at all how animals communicate. I speak to Serge by humming even though his room is two doors down. He knows my language, came from a deciduous forest in Maine, and once helped a black bear find a suitable den for hibernation. Because he's mostly human, he doesn't need to hibernate. He used to stay at the St. Francis Shelter when the snows came. Like me, he dislikes human food except for berries and nuts, an occasional bird. Carol brings me granola in a plastic container. Glass is better because it's shiny but the Strongmen won't allow it. They are used to making the rules, even ones that make no sense like when Carol can visit, and how much time I'm allowed in the sunroom where I can watch the jays raid the birdfeeder, see the cherry trees shriek into blossom. Carol always tells me I'll be home soon, and I think of my favorite maple tree. I don't wound it like the people who insert a metal tap in the tree's torso, hang a bucket to collect the blood. They don't understand that it is the sap that keeps the tree strong. It's important to keep one's fluids to oneself.

"Susan. Time for your pill."

Eliza is a Strongman even though she's female. She wears their uniform of blue cotton with white whispery shoes. I know she wants to read my dreams so she can understand the language of plants and animals but I don't let her. I've learned how to stick the pill in my left back molar, the one with a cavity. When I go to the loo, I spit it in the toilet and flush, watch it spiral down into the septic system but I worry about fish losing their dreams.

I open my mouth like a good robot. Eliza put me on Step Five because I'm one of the well-behaved ones. I don't tie my sheets into knots or spit out mashed potatoes. As long as I can have some nuts and berries, I am quiet as a snake. It is April and soon they'll open up the courtyard. Carol can take me outside and maybe through the gate to Keeper's Park down the street. You have to be a Six to go there but all it takes is opening my mouth and sitting in the semi-circle when Strongman Dr. Benton comes in.

"Click, clack, click. How do you feel about that, Susan?"

"Click, clack, clack. I feel fine, Dr. Benton."

There's a dogwood sapling outside the window that has been trying to get my attention. She shakes her greening limbs and tells me stories about the vole that lives underground. I promise to save her some water from the pink plastic pitcher by my bed so her buds will open like promises.

Carol joined the human race at seven. She was never one of us but it's safer that way. She speaks their language so they let me go places with her. They punch in a series of numbers on the little metal door and then more numbers on the bigger door until it opens to the land of unfenced trees and boxy houses.

"My mother needs fresh air. Do you think I could take her to the park on Saturday?"

"Click, clack, click. Group goals, individual goals, Step Five."

"Great. I know she'll make Six by then. She's so pale, it will be good for her to get outside."

Kurt spoke that language, too. He kicked me out early. At first it felt dark and strange because I didn't fit into his forest, buried my roots beyond the park, next to the hiking trail where Carol got lost one day.

"Susan, why weren't you keeping an eye on her?"

Kurt had a kind face, promised to keep me safe when we met on the bench at Creeley Park. I told him about clear cutting, how they were mowing down my relatives with chainsaws, and he laughed, called me an environmentalist, a *treehugger*. He couldn't see the depth of the cuts, the muscles, and all those severed limbs strewn by the path.

"I love how you're passionate about this, Susan. I've met so many people who don't care about the earth."

I married him because he promised there would be flowers and a trip to see the redwoods in Oregon. We had pink petunias and blue and yellow pansies in ceramic pots so we could plant them outside Kurt's house later. Kurt built me a little wooden bench in the garden, just like the one in the park.

"You can watch your roses and columbine now. You're a funny woman, Susan."

Then he thought I wasn't funny anymore, sometime after Carol was born. Babies can understand all languages. That's why they don't talk; they're too busy listening. Once they start to speak, they become self-absorbed like the rest of the humans. Their words start to click and clack, and they talk about weather and what kind of poison is best for getting rid of dandelions and ants. I wanted to keep Carol away from all that but Kurt took her from me, put her in the red rectangular building with painted handprints on the wall, and children who brought their lunches in plastic boxes, didn't understand what the trees and dogs had to say.

Kurt doesn't visit me anymore. He married Adrienne and they moved from the deciduous forest to a place called Stamford. Everything is oblong and gray there. Carol calls it *the city*. She's grown, lives with Seymour, her Irish setter.

When I'm on Step Six, the Strongmen will let her bring Seymour to visit me and we can talk about where he's digging and what the earth smells like in April after a rain. Dogs like to talk about smells since their noses are so close to the ground. If allowed to roam, they reminisce about all the animals that have wandered in their path and I feel less lonely listening to them. Kurt thought that barking was the dog just taking a breath, a sharp intake of air but I know better. Barking is conversation, a complicated social network that dogs develop to expand the confines of their yards and homes. Sometimes they escape, arrange to meet by the river or down the street, warn each other about the dreaded animal control officer with his green truck. Leash laws are incarceration for canines. I want to destroy all the leashes and short-circuit the invisible fences.

"I have to get an invisible fence for Seymour. They have a leash law in New Fordham now. A little boy was bitten by a Pit Bull and now everyone has to restrain their dogs. I know how you hate that, Mother."

Pit Bulls are angry because people fear them. They don't want to argue or bite. Little boys and girls tease dogs because they weren't taught to respect animals, and a Pit Bull is like a wrestler. Broad chested and muscular, they don't have to put up with anything. Some days I wish I had more Pit Bull in me.

When I make it to Level Six, they hold a party for me. There are cupcakes with pink icing and nuts and berries. I don't eat the cupcakes but I drink three cups of a sugary punch the color of cranberries.

When Carol arrives with Seymour, I'm already dressed in my walking clothes, complicated buttons and zippered trousers. It's silly but I need them to think I know how to look like them.

"You look wonderful, Mother. I like that blue fleece on you. It matches your eyes."

You never hear dogs or trees talk like this. They don't waste language like humans do, saving it to nudge each other or warn of weather or people. Carol drives a red car with gray seats. I buckle my seatbelt even though it makes me feel like the restraints are around me. I know Carol won't drive unless I do this because there's a law. Humans like to make laws about how fast you can go, what you need to do when you get to one of their lights or signs, and where you can park.

When we get to the park, I see all my friends lined up to welcome me. The curly maple has grown taller in my absence. Seymour nuzzles my hand because he knows what's it's like to only see the outdoors through a square pane of a window or an electrified plot of land. Carol lets him off his leash so he can run. He pees on the side of one tree and then another to let his friends know he's been here. When Carol takes out the picnic basket, the one with juice, nuts, berries, and some sort of seedy breed with nut butter, I practice the pill-in-the-molar kind of pretending.

"Delicious lunch, Carol."

"Thanks, Mother. I think you're doing so much better."

Seymour looks at me with his golden eyes, makes a little gurgling sound in the back of his throat and I hum in response.

When I stand up, at least a half dozen trees bend to point out the path ahead. Two red squirrels wait for me by the pines; I saved peanuts and sunflower seeds in my pocket. Now I know why they call these shoes sneakers. While Carol is pulling out the Gala apples, I make a run for it, swooshing over the pine needles and dirt beds, my eye on a patch of sky tangled up in the hair of the Douglas fir trees. The wind gives me a push and I propel myself faster and faster, watching the smallest squirrel vault from one tree branch to another, poking his head against the bark. Carol is calling me, *click, clack, click, clack* but it's not a language I speak anymore.

The White Man

after Stevens and Shelley

One must have a mind of power
to regard the steel and the thew
of the towers slathered in gold;

and have been master a long time
to behold the masses shagged numb,
the rivers hushed in the distant smother

of the January rain; and not to think
of any misery in the sound of the wind,
in the sound of many leaves,

yellow, and black, and hectic red,
which is the sound of the land
owned and disowned in the same fraught place

by the pale man, who hears the springs and summers
of others and, helpless himself, beholds
the whiteness that is not his and the whiteness that is.

Daniel W. Thompson

His Last

It was July so it was hot and so were his fingers. The paper grew wet against their moisture. An itchy heat, like sunburned skin aching for relief. He had rolled the cigarette between his thumb and forefinger for thirty minutes, lifting it every couple minutes to smell its musty leaves. The sweet aroma cut open his salivary glands and he wiped the corners of his mouth. The thought, no one will know, pecked on his brain. This one, he promised himself, would be the last one. Just like the one this morning after Sandy left for work. And the one last night after Sandy went to bed. One more last one, but god dammit, definitely the last one. Just then their brown lab, George, snapped through the dog door, and John dropped the cigarette onto the decking boards. It rolled into a crack and lodged half-way. The fire inside turned to ice. He had crushed his last pack of cigarettes leaving this one literally his last, at least for the night. John curled his broad body over the stuck stick and tried prying it out with his pinky but the beefy finger was too swollen in the heat. He knew much of any movement could shift the weathered boards and swallow everything. His cigarette. His sixty-two years. Three children. A wife of almost forty years. The insurance company. Three club championships. It all hung in the balance, suspended over that dark crack. He'd have broken the bones in his hands to squeeze a finger into that crack. But thankfully he remembered the grill spatula hanging on the deck post and gently lifted the wet and dirty cigarette from the perilous edge. His hands shook so badly he had to set the cigarette on the grill counter and find his breath. His lungs rattled. His nose whistled. His ears burned. Since he was fourteen John, a product of southern Virginia's tobacco culture, had smoked. Then, at the age of fifty-nine, he came home from the golf course one evening and collapsed against the front steps. A quadruple bypass surgery later and the doctor's prescription was simple. For life, never smoke again.

Except telling a man of almost sixty years to stop doing what he had done twenty times a day for 17,000 days, wouldn't work simply. To his credit, John tried. John failed. And he tried and failed and tried and failed. And he stood over his last wrinkled Marlboro Red like George over his well-chewed bone. He'd never part with it. He'd never quit and he dammed the gods other people believed in, letting temptation wash over him like a steam bath. He grabbed the worn silver zippo from his jeans pocket and raised the cigarette to his mouth where a silver bead of sweat lined his upper lip. Scar tissue, tangled in his chest, squeezed against his lungs. The long, purple scar bisecting his chest pulsed. It seemed to reach through his sticky golf shirt and indecision crawled over his body. John shook his head, then wrung his hand. Death wasn't worth it. He said it aloud, death wasn't worth it. He rolled the cigarette between his fingers. He flipped open and shut the zippo. He flipped open and shut the zippo. He rolled the cigarette. Then, as if controlled by another man, the crooked, dangling cigarette lit and rose to his lips and John collapsed to his knees, coughing out the exhaustion.

Assessment Rubric

In the manner of my people
I hereby commodify
my life's value:

Given an investment
heavily front-loaded, I paid dearly
those early years in health woes
and human misery,
but year by steady year
my assets grew.

With interest
compounding and no fees
left to pay, at last I'm free
to reap the benefits.

No longer broke,
now just broken.

Horn Man

Harold Washington unfolded his three-legged metal stool and set it down on the sidewalk. The sun was still hiding behind the second story of the old brick building across Martin Luther King, Jr. Boulevard. Harold hoped to collect enough change in the next few hours to buy a cup of fancy coffee at the new café on the corner.

He lowered himself onto the stool, his long thin legs folded up and then spread out to the side. He used his elegant slender fingers to unlock a battered brown case which he'd set next to him on the ground.

The lid lifted easily. As it did, Harold got a whiff of what he liked to call *old air,* a sour smell the faded and stained purple cloth had soaked up over the years. Harold had lost nearly everything in his life: wives, children, a three-bedroom house, untold apartments and cars, including his favorite, a sleek silver Mercedes sports car. But one thing he'd managed to hold onto. That one thing was his horn.

People who lived in the neighborhood, folks who went to the restaurants and bars on MLK Boulevard or who waited under and outside the shelter for the Number Seven, Number Thirty-Three or the Seventy-Five bus, all knew Harold. Or rather, they knew the guy everyone called the *Horn Man.* He looked battered, as so many folks on the sidewalks did these days. And while no one had any idea of his age, most people would have simply said the Horn Man was an old guy.

Everyone would agree. The Horn Man was never without that hat. That hat, like its owner, had seen better days. The color was gray, a smooth silver gray, and it had a wide matching ribbon above the brim. It was impossible to look at the Horn Man in that hat and not imagine the man he had once been, dressed in a sleek suit that matched, a smooth gabardine much too refined to shine.

Harold lifted a silver saxophone from the case and fingered the keys. He ran his tongue the length of the reed, getting it moist, at the same moment he pressed the keys to loosen them. What no one could see as the Horn Man sat on his stool was that he was slowly sliding away from the sidewalk, with its soda stains and crushed cigarette butts and dried mud, into the place of musical ecstasy. The fingering, wetting the reed and slightly blowing into the horn was certainly necessary for him to play. But it also happened to be Harold's way of bowing to the god of jazz, the one who let Harold enter the only place he felt happy and safe.

No one knew where Harold had come from or even where he slept. They didn't know if he'd ever been married or had children or anything like that. What they did know was that Harold could play the tenor saxophone like a man who knew his way around an instrument. One neighborhood woman, Ella Johnson, who liked to say she'd been around the block with too many no-good men to recall, figured she knew everything she needed to know about the Horn Man.

"He got himself all messed up with them drugs," Ella said one morning, while she was getting her hair straightened and cut and styled at the new salon down the block.

"How you know that?" asked Leticia Williams, the owner of the salon.

"I had me a man once, looked just like Horn Man. He was getting himself gigs all over the place, in Oakland and New Orleans. Even in New York. He was fine, that man, and he sure could play that horn. Make you wanna cry.

"Then he got messed up with them drugs," Ella went on. "That was the end of the music. End of everything."

"But thas a different man, Ella," Leticia argued. "How you know the same thing happened to the Horn Man?"

"I just know," Ella said, and turned her head to the side, to see how her hairdo looked from that angle.

On this particular Tuesday morning, the day dawned warm and dry. Harold was glad. He spent a good ten minutes fingering the keys of his horn, licking the reed and blowing a bit of air into the horn from time to time. He was asking permission to enter the jazz place. As always, he worried that the god of music might not let him enter.

It must have been Harold Washington's lucky day because the moment he blew hard into that instrument, a note as pure as a baby's breath drifted into the air. Harold started then, playing that heartbreaking tune from Porgy and Bess, "I Loves You, Porgy." The way Harold played brought out the heat and dampness contained in every note, slowing the tempo down in the process.

As Harold blew his saxophone, the music allowed him to leave the sidewalk and travel back through the years. He saw himself once again in the early days of his musical career, standing under a circle of white light, looking slick in a new silver-gray suit that matched his hat. The club was packed with couples at small round tables lit by candlelight, the women wearing dresses that sparkled and high heels that clicked across the floor when they walked. Every woman in that club had a secret desire to go home with the saxophone player and ditch the man she'd come with, simply because of the way Harold caressed those notes.

Harold had a small combo behind him— a piano player, guitar player, drummer and a guy on the bass. The group was simply called, The Harold Washington Quintet. In the audience that night, nursing the same glass of Chivas Regal, was a guy from New York, scouting out new jazz talent to record and promote. So far, he was liking what he heard.

The morning crowd started to walk by Harold Washington there on the sidewalk. No matter what Ella Johnson thought, she nevertheless admired the Horn Man's music and considered it her Christian duty to help him out. On her way to the bus stop, she dropped a crisp one dollar bill into the Horn Man's cup and said, "Mornin'." She barely whispered the word, mostly because she didn't want to disturb him while he blew his horn.

After leaving that dollar in Horn Man's cup, Ella checked her watch.

"I gotta coupla' minutes," Ella whispered now.

She stood off to the side and listened to Horn Man play a tune from Porgy and Bess she recognized. The thought ran through her mind, as it sometimes did when she heard the Horn Man play, that it was a dammed shame. She always said that at the beauty parlor when the women began to talk about the man who played the tenor sax so well on Martin Luther King, Jr. Boulevard.

"A dammed shame," Ella had said just the previous Saturday. "Good man like that. Man with so much talent. A dammed shame."

The other women in the salon echoed what Ella had just said, nodding their heads, some covered with metal curler rods and others with their hair hanging wet and straight. Like Ella, the other women in the beauty parlor had been around the block too many times with good black men gone bad.

"It's like a curse," Ella said.

Leticia Williams, who'd found Jesus a while back and turned to preaching in addition to doing hair, said, "They done givin' in to the Devil. They need to turn back to God."

"Maybe so," Ella said. "Maybe so."

And then Ella started remembering that fine man she'd fallen for years back when she was forty pounds lighter, and could make a pair of three and a half-inch heels and a short snug dress shout.

His name was Earl. Earl Jackson. She had met him at a club. (Oh, what was the name of the club?) The Be-Bop. That's what they called it. Gone now, like all the places that had music back then. Boy, the street was hoppin'. You could have gone in half a dozen places and heard jazz any night of the week. Even Sunday. Ella and her girlfriends used to get all dolled up. Ella thought about it now, how much fun they had getting dressed up, standing in front of her closet looking through the dresses—picking out a red one that sparkled or a royal blue. Or if she was feeling especially daring, a bright pink that came down low in the front.

She wore the red one that night she, Mavis and Winnie stepped into the Be-Bop. They didn't even get there until eleven o'clock because otherwise they'd be too early. From Ella's apartment on Fifteenth Street, they walked over to the club right there on MLK. You could do that in those days because the neighborhood wasn't like it had gotten these days. Young guys didn't drive around in cars shooting bullets at each another. No. Guys drove slow to look at girls, that's what.

And people went out to the clubs to hear music. Ella and her girlfriends sure liked good music. But the clubs were where they went to meet men and that's why they waited to drop into the Be-Bop until eleven.

They liked to sit up front near the stage because the men that appealed to them most were in the band. When the dancing started, Ella and her girlfriends were in the right place for men to come over and ask them to dance.

Earl Jackson played the horn. The night she first set her eyes on him at the Be-Bop, he had on one of those long African shirts, bright green and purple and yellow. The man had skin the color of hot pulled caramel and a small Afro. He wore a cloth cap on his head that went along with his African style.

Ella could feel Earl Jackson's eyes on her in between tunes as he looked out at the crowd. His gaze felt wet and she tried not to act like she knew it. Instead, she turned her head away from that smooth sax player and pretended to admire the other musicians. Earl Jackson's gaze followed. She could feel his eyes all over her breasts.

"Silly to think about that man now," Ella muttered to herself.

"What's that?" Leticia asked, as she worked on Ella's hairdo.

"Oh, nothing. I was just remembering. A long time ago. Not worth thinking about, that's what."

Standing off to the side listening to Horn Man play, Ella couldn't help but go back to that time. She didn't realize that the Horn Man had also left the sidewalk bordering Martin Luther King, Junior Boulevard. In his mind, he was back in that New Orleans club when the man from the record company sat at a table up front, barely touching his Chivas Regal (because he was working after all and didn't want to cloud his judgment). Fingering the keys for the tune he played that night, Harold Washington slid right back into that life. He could feel the man he was then. A man, yes, and that felt awfully nice.

Harold stepped up to the microphone at the end of that tune and said, "We're gonna take a short break. Don't go away."

And with that he set his horn down in the gleaming silver stand next to the microphone. He pulled a folded white handkerchief from his back pocket, lifted it and wiped the sweat from his forehead, cheeks and his chin, before returning the still-folded cloth to his pocket. He stepped down from the stage. Because he felt someone's gaze on him, he turned in that direction. A short, bald white man sitting at a table up front nodded. As Harold nodded back, he was thinking how much he wanted a drink because his throat was dry.

That's how it began. Many times, Harold traced back in his mind the way he'd gone from a musician who only wanted to play music every chance he got, to a man who craved success and something else. The record deal brought the kind of money Harold had never imagined before. And, yes, he wanted to taste the good life. And taste it he did. Before long, that's what mattered more than the music. Tasting, tasting, tasting. More than Sherilynn, his wife. More even than his two kids.

If anyone had asked, Harold couldn't have explained when his life began to unravel. He didn't remember the half of it. He'd developed a thirst he couldn't quench. At one time, the music took him every place he cared to go. But now he needed the drugs and booze. Sometimes, Harold got so high he couldn't find the notes anymore. The gigs dried up, and Harold's wife said she'd had enough. A dozen years or more drifted by while Harold slept in doorways, playing his horn for spare change to buy bottles of cheap sweet wine.

Ella needed to get over to the bus stop and head downtown. Yet something made her stop. She'd been listening to Horn Man all these years, dropping a dollar or two into his cup, saying, "Mornin'," or "Evenin'," but never asking anything. Today she had the urge to change.

When Harold finished playing and before he had the chance to start another tune, Ella asked, "How'd you learn to play like that?"

She turned toward Horn Man and noticed that he looked confused. Ella waited a moment for him to answer.

When she didn't get a response, she said, "You hear what I ask you?"

Horn Man sat for a moment staring into space, as if the answer to Ella's question hung in the air.

"Yes, I heard you," he said, not turning his head.

"Then you must not want to tell me."

Horn Man thought about the question and saw himself once again as a young boy. Yes, he remembered. Sitting at a small round table with his mama all dolled up, his mama's perfume making him sneeze. He was shy and short at the time, his legs dangling high above the floor. His mama ordered a sweet fruit juice drink for him and he leaned down over the table to sip it from a straw.

"Clap for your daddy," he heard his mama tell him and he clapped his hands hard, like he did in church when the choir really got going. His daddy blew that horn on the stage and little Harold felt the notes surge through his heart, making him shiver and almost cry.

"My daddy taught me," Harold said to Ella at last.

Harold hadn't seen his father going on twenty years, the night he heard a loud insistent voice coming from somewhere in the dark club. By that time, Harold had his own quintet and was beginning to make a name for himself. He hadn't noticed the man sitting at a table off to the side until halfway through the first set. They'd just finished playing that Charlie Parker tune, "A Night in Tunisia," when out of the dark a too-loud voice said, "Thas my son."

At first, Harold didn't pay attention. But after the group started in on the next tune, somewhere into his first solo, Harold heard it again.

"Thas my son."

By now, he knew. But he kept right on playing.

The next song was interrupted with louder declarations from that side of the room. Yes, sometimes customers got a little carried away by the music and let their pleasure be known. But this was something else.

At the end of the tune, Harold let the other musicians know that he wanted to cut the first set short. He turned back around and leaned into the microphone. In a deep low voice, Harold practically whispered into the microphone, "We're gonna take a short break. Stick around."

He set his horn in the silver stand and didn't bother to wipe the sweat off his forehead. As he stepped down from the stage, he recalled the last time he'd seen his father.

His mother had wanted to surprise her husband at the club. She was pregnant then, her belly so big she had trouble getting past the tightly packed tables and chairs in the dark.

They sat down at a table three rows back from the front. Harold's father was blowing his horn. Before his mother even ordered Harold's sweet sticky fruit drink, the song ended. Harold's father leaned into the microphone. "We'll be right back."

Harold's father stepped off the stage in the middle of the club, almost directly in front of the table where Harold and his very pregnant mother sat three rows back. Harold waited for his father to walk over and kiss his mama and give Harold a big grin. But instead Harold watched as his father leaned down and kissed another woman smack on the lips.

As if the kiss wasn't bad enough, the woman got up from the table where she'd been sitting right in front of the stage, and Harold's father sat down. Dressed in a body-hugging red satin dress, the woman lowered herself onto Harold's father's lap.

She wrapped her arms around Harold's father's neck. They kissed again. This time, the embrace was noticeably longer.

Harold's mama reached across the table and grabbed her young son's arm, yanking him off his chair.

"Let's go, son," she whispered, her voice raspy and harsh.

~~~

"Thas my son. Thas my son." The voice could not be ignored. Harold tried to weave his way through the crowded club to the bar. The voice got more insistent and louder.

Eddie, the bouncer, walked over.

"I'll go walk him out," Eddie said.

Harold looked at Eddie. He thought for a moment about the last time he'd seen his father, standing on the sidewalk, surrounded by his clothes in haphazard piles. Harold's mama had tossed the clothes out the window that morning.

"No, Eddie," Harold said, shaking his head. "I'll handle it."

Up until that night, he had managed to believe that the ball of anger and hurt, as well as the disappointment and dread he'd carried around inside him all the years since his father vanished from his life didn't exist. But after escorting his drunk father out of the club, something happened to Harold. Without the least provocation, anger would mix with hurt and fear to flood his mind, making it impossible for Harold to think. He lashed out at his wife and kids. He screamed at the other musicians. And then he grabbed a drink and later a needle, both of which he claimed *mellowed him out.*

One hot and humid July night, Harold came home from playing at an after-hours club and found his wife and two children gone. His wife's side of the closet was empty, except for two bare wire hangers dangling several inches apart. She hadn't bothered to leave Harold a note, saying where she'd gone.

The only way Harold knew how to live with the silence his wife had left him in the apartment was to get high and play his horn. Some nights he got so lost in the music, he forgot to show up at the club. Several times on stage, Harold misplaced the tune he and the other musicians were playing and he took off alone on a different one.

Not surprisingly, musicians quit the group and the gigs began to dry up. When Harold couldn't pay the rent two months in a row, the landlord posted an eviction notice on the front door and moved Harold's bed and clothes out to the sidewalk. At first, Harold stayed with friends, making sure not to linger in any one place for long. When he wore out his welcome, he started sleeping under the freeway overpass.

One by one, Harold's teeth fell out. By that time, he looked at least ten years older than he'd gotten. And to get by, he set himself up each morning on Martin Luther King, Junior Boulevard, where he became known for how well he played jazz standards on the tenor saxophone.

Ella had missed two buses while she'd been listening to the Horn Man. It might have been the warm sultry air or the memories that Horn Man's music had dredged up, but Ella was being caressed by the days when she could still attract a man as fine as Earl Jackson. Yes, she should have left a half-hour ago for her job but Ella wanted to hold on a little while longer to that former time in her mind. She had already concocted a story to tell her supervisor. For now, she was enjoying the music, the warm breeze that hadn't yet turned hot, and daydreaming about a trip she might take to Jamaica, after losing a good twenty pounds or so.

Harold was surprised that he didn't mind so much having this woman standing next to him while he played his horn. Other times, he preferred his space, being alone and separate from people. But today, he found this woman's lingering beside him on the sidewalk comforting.

And, yes, he lost himself in the tunes and for a time left the sidewalk completely. As he lifted up from that cracked and stained concrete, littered with cigarette butts and crushed waxed paper drink cups, the years fell away. He was once again a young man with a full set of beautiful white teeth. He'd gotten back his youthful hair—dark, thick, and nappy, instead of thin yellow-gray. The lines etching his face miraculously went away.

But each time he played the last note of a tune, Harold couldn't avoid returning to the sidewalk. At least when he did, that woman was still standing there, as if she didn't have another place in the world she'd rather be.

Lake Eerie is the Shallowest of All the Great Lakes

Ice cream drips down my hand. Vanilla-covered knuckles clutch a waffle cone because the booth was out of chocolate. Those last six chocolate scoops walk away, three boys holding sugar cones and licking two scoops each as they run through the crowd.

But vanilla will be all right, Vanessa told me. It's still ice cream, four scoops for us to share. Now we just have to find our bench, and we can turn back time to five years ago, relive our first date all over again.

Vanessa drags me by my ice-cream-free hand past organ music and screaming kids riding merry-go-round horses. Past couples wearing matching tie-dyed shirts, stuffing fried pickles in their mouths, and holding hands as they climb into Ferris wheel carts.

Vanessa stops walking. "Here it is. This is where it all began. For a minute, I thought it wasn't going to be here."

It's a simple bench with wooden planks running across the seat and up the back. Black metal armrests run up each side, too hard and uncomfortable to be allowed to use the word "rest" in their name. With each of its four legs bolted into the concrete below, the bench isn't going anywhere, even if it wants to, I could tell Vanessa, but I don't. And even if it could get up to leave, I would say, it truly doesn't want to go anywhere else, but she'd probably still not believe me.

I fall onto the bench, and Vanessa hops onto my lap, momentarily knocking the wind out of me. The bench offers an empty seat next to me, unlike five years ago, when an elderly couple sat next to me holding hands, and Vanessa simply "went for it" and sat on my lap, cementing her unannounced title as "girlfriend" before the ending of our first date.

The bench sits under Mega Corkscrew Twist, the two and a half minutes of upside down, head-jerking, dipping, bending, and body-flipping around a twirling track that has left me with a whiplash migraine.

Just past the ride, for miles we have a clear view of Lake Erie. The sun is just over the horizon of the hazy blue water, about to set for the evening. We sat here five years ago after walking up and down the park all day, riding every coaster we passed at least two times each. Coming here was Vanessa's idea, saying we should do something different than the typical dinner-and-a-movie first-date stuff. Something the *guy* would enjoy. Before we even finished riding the first coaster, it was already my best first date ever.

We walked until our feet were sore, talked until our mouths hurt from laughing. Then we sat right here on this bench, watching the sun setting over the lake. The water looked so deeply blue and calm, like a mirror showing the sun's bright reflection to give us double our sunset money's worth. Then I leaned in and kissed her. It lasted for all of three seconds, that one kiss, but that was enough.

Vanessa moved in with me three months later. Her lease expired, and she finished the mere formality of throwing away expired food from her refrigerator, as everything from her toothbrush to her Social Security card had already made it to my place.

For those first few months, Vanessa cooked candlelight dinners with soft music playing in the background every night. She'd bake homemade lasagna with *both* sausage and ground meat baked into the sauce, all because on our first date, I told her my grandmother used to make it that way. After that first year, I started having to buy pants two sizes bigger. But she always said she didn't mind—it was simply more of me she could love.

What guy couldn't love that kind of love?

It's been five years since we first sat on this bench, the sun setting and rising 1,725 times since then. And just now are we finding ourselves coming back.

~~~

Vanessa picked out my outfit for today—the same khaki shorts and black polo shirt I wore on that first date. She must have dug into the back of my closet to find the shorts and shirt, as I can't remember wearing them in years. The shorts are shorter than I remember, stopping six inches above my knees, revealing way too much of my pale inner thighs. And a back covered in crackling bacon would keep me cooler than this weaving of black 100 percent polyester. After eight hours walking up and down the park, who I wouldn't kill right now to strip naked and dive into the fountain with all the kids dumped off by parents looking to escape to a hotdog or a beer or a Valium.

A group of screams roar toward us, as the roller coaster cars twist upside down just over our heads.

I lift the ice cream cone to block my eyes from the sun, trying to shelter my still-ringing, roller-coaster-induced migraine.

Vanessa watches the cars corkscrew over our heads across the orange track. "You used to love this roller coaster. You made me ride it with you over and over last time, and it never gave you a headache."

I rub my temples with my free hand. "I think they made it faster. Or they added some extra twists and turns that weren't there before."

"It's the same bolts and metal it was then. Nothing is different."

"Felt different," I say, staring at the river of vanilla dripping down my hand.

Her sandals occupy the empty space on the bench. Those extravagant black, fettuccine-thick straps that run over the tops of her feet and around her heel, then origami-wrap up her mid calf before being tied off. The straps dig into her calves, tight enough to stay in place, and tight enough to cut off blood flow to all lower extremities. The heels require a stepladder to get in them. Last time, she strutted up and down the park for eight hours, never taking them off, letting me stare at her toned, tanned legs. But today, she groaned and winced with each step for the first three hours, finally surrendering and going barefoot since lunch.

Cutoff jean shorts so short the frayed denim doubles as underwear. Vanessa painted on her tank top this morning, the white polyester fibers clinging to each other for dear life over her curvy stomach. When she put on her throwback outfit this morning, Vanessa said, "I think the dryer must have shrunk it," leaving me nodding my head in agreement, never bringing up the clothes haven't changed—what the clothes are covering has changed. Sitting here now, she's a hard sneeze away from the park instituting the *No Shoes, No Shirt, No Service* policy.

She pushes her freshly dyed blond hair (matching her dyed blond hair from five years ago, and bookending five years of her natural brown hair in between) over her shoulder, licking away at the ice cream. Her tongue swipes back and forth, putting dents into scoop number four, and leaving scoops two and three in a race to see which one will drip to my elbow first. A vanilla goatee covers her chin. Commercial breaks separate my turn to lick, like she's passive-aggressively punishing me by letting me hold the cone, but never letting me eat it.

Vanessa stops licking. "What time is it? Is it almost time for the sunset?"

"Not yet," I say.

"You're still going to surprise me, right? Like last time. I don't want to see it coming, and then you kiss me. Just as the sun is setting over the water."

"I know," I say. "I will."

I even have the Chap Stick at the ready in my pocket.

She says, "That was my favorite part about the kiss—the surprise. It was so spontaneous, and I knew it meant we'd be together and happy forever. We can have that moment again, just you watch. It can be just like it was before."

Vanessa looks at her watch. "What time is the sunset tonight?"

~ ~ ~

We get college interns every summer at work. "Summer associates," we call them. Young students barely over twenty years old who need internship hours to build their résumés for law school. They are normally fairly knowledgeable in field, yet wholly fresh-faced to life outside of dormitories, ramen noodles, and keg parties. Never once did I look twice at any of them when they spent all day doing legal research, document review, or coming back from coffee runs.

But this past summer, I looked twice.

Her name was Alex. She was a junior in college, with long, straight auburn hair and three freckles on the tip of her nose. She had a pair of wide blue eyes that never seemed to blink, making her stare feel hypnotic. And she smiled when she said "good morning," instinctively, every day, like she truly meant it—"Today will be a good morning." That kind of optimism was infectious, especially in such a boring law office as mine.

I'm only thirty-one, so I wasn't too old to know noticing her was wrong. But I'm old enough that it still felt that way.

She had never even heard of Radiohead, for God's sake. Or Weezer, R.E.M., or any other band I listened to in college. A decade's difference felt like too much.

But still, that smile.

The other interns all sat around the corner, at a group table, out of my eyeline, out of my memory. But Alex sat at a desk just five feet away from me, just out of my reach.

Over her twelve weeks interning, our lunches seemed to always overlap in the cafeteria. I'd be eating some extravagant three-course meal Vanessa made me the night before—leftover meatloaf with mashed potatoes and homemade gravy. Or spaghetti, meatballs, and fresh Parmesan cheese sprinkled over top.

Alex always ate whatever mishmash of food she could scrap out of her intern-salary-bare cupboards—yogurt sprinkled with dried cranberries. Or just the endless slices of leftover cold pizza from the night before.

Those thirty-minute lunches were a youthful recharge for me. And in return, I spent most of that time trying to convince her to stop listening to whatever nonmusic her generation listened to—I still haven't figured out if Jimmy Eat World is the name of the lead singer or just the band itself.

At the end of the summer, I knew agreeing to go with her to the Pearl Jam concert was a mistake. But lying to Vanessa, saying I was meeting guys out for drinks after work was an even bigger mistake.

Standing in the crowd at the concert, looking down at Alex smiling up at me, I pictured Vanessa sitting at home, baking another dinner for me—always making extras, for my lunch the next day. She'd be waiting up for me, like she does whenever I go out with the guys, ready to ask me who won the game, even if she didn't know what sport was playing that night.

I told myself I needed just one kiss. It would last for three seconds, and that would be enough to quench my thirst the rest of my life. I'd plea temporary insanity from the affections of a younger woman, hoping for a first-offense misdemeanor punishable with only temporary sleeping-on-the-couch probation. I knew it was wrong, but I convinced myself I needed that one kiss.

Our lips touched. It lasted for all of three seconds, that one kiss, and that was enough.

But our second kiss lasted for hours, all the way to back at her place, until the next morning.

~~~

Another couple walks up and stops in front of us. His receding hairline says "you're too young to be balding but tough shit" when he looks in the mirror. But at least his khaki shorts hang to the tops of his knees, hiding any and all pale man-thigh.

His girlfriend sports an outfit that wouldn't get her arrested in thirty-one states with one quick tear of fabric. Gray cotton shorts emphasize tanned legs, and an orange tank top shows the picture of an alligator underneath the words "University of Florida," while exposing her red, sunburned shoulders. A ponytail pulls back auburn hair, with a few dangling pieces falling out, running over her deep-blue eyes.

I notice all of this about her. Then I turn my head and look away, so I can stop noticing.

The couple holds hands, staring at Vanessa's sandals taking up the free seat on the bench.

Vanessa looks the girl up and down, and then she *doesn't* move the sandals away.

The couple sits on the curb across from us, their butts resting on that two-inch slab of concrete dividing the walkway from the grass.

The boyfriend holds an ice cream cone in his hand. Two scoops. Mint chocolate chip (in a sugar cone—my preference, but Vanessa likes waffle cones better, so I let her choose today, and now, apparently, forever). They take turns licking, a well-oiled machine of back and forth, their tongues swirling on cue, starting where the ice cream meets the cone, going clockwise up to the top.

Vanessa stares at the girl the entire time, every few seconds nudging deeper into my lap, wrapping her arm tighter over my shoulder.

I push Vanessa off my lap, jumping off the bench. "I have to go to the bathroom."

Vanessa says, "You're coming right back, right?"

"Of course," I say. "Where else would I go?"

I know it's the wrong thing to say the moment it leaves my mouth.

Vanessa says, "Just make sure you're back before sunset. And remember to make it a surprise. I want to be surprised when you kiss me. Just like last time."

I walk down the pathway, wiping my sticky hand over the top of my khaki shorts, passing the bathrooms, disappearing into the crowd.

~~~

Screams promising a winner every time fill the humid air. Bells and whistles shoot off with each basketball falling through a hoop, each dart hitting the bull's-eye in the middle of a golden star. People hand money to workers in blue uniforms to shoot toy guns, toss beanbags, and run around clutching giant teddy bears they spent fifty bucks and two hours trying to win.

I walk through them all, to the end of the park, right to a brick wall with a sign that reads: "If you can read this, then all the fun is behind you."

Turning and walking back through the crowd, I see the girl from the curb earlier, now standing next to the bathroom. She stands alone, holding only the last bite of her sugar cone, every ounce of mint chocolate chip completely licked away.

She stares out over the fence, watching the waves on the lake crash over the banks.

Her name is probably Sam. Or Peyton. She probably spends her Friday nights eating greasy cheeseburgers with draft beer at the only Irish bar in town. She has a loft downtown, filled only with bags of chamomile tea in the cupboards and walls plastered with concert posters from her travels all across the country. She eats Chinese food with chopsticks. Nothing about her is especially fascinating, yet everything somehow still is.

I realize I'm now standing shoulder-to-shoulder with this girl. I hadn't even realized I walked up next to her.

She turns away from the water, looking at me.

I say the first thing that comes to mind. "Did you know that of all the Great Lakes, Lake Erie is the shallowest?"

It's the same thing I said to Vanessa when we sat on our bench together five years ago.

"You don't say." She smiles back at me. "Does that mean if I fell off a boat in the middle of the lake, I'd be able to touch?"

I say, "Only if you know the exact right place to fall out. Then you'd have the best seat in the house for every sunset."

From behind me, I hear a voice say, "Hey buddy—win something for the pretty girl."

I turn around and see a kid standing inside a tent, wearing a blue uniform and a trickle of peach fuzz above his upper lip. He juggles three white softballs.

She looks at me, and then she looks back at the boy. "We're not together. I have a boyfriend, you know. He's just inside the bathroom, but he'll be back in a minute."

"Knock off all seven jugs and win the grand prize." The kid points up to a row of four-foot-tall, neon-pink stuffed elephants sitting on the top shelf, above a round tray holding seven stacked jugs.

"That's all right," I say. "It doesn't mean a guy still can't win a woman a prize."

I hand the kid a five-spot and wait for change that doesn't come. He tosses me the three balls.

I wind up and throw the first ball, knocking off three of the seven jugs.

Earlier this year, Vanessa forgave me for my summer indiscretion. It took two weeks of all-night talking sessions, and Vanessa analyzing what could make me do such a thing to her after all our years together. Ultimately, I convinced her it was a onetime mistake, temporary relationship insanity from the affections of a younger woman, and I served out my first-offense week of sleeping-on-the-couch probation.

Even I know I got off easy.

I wind up and throw the second ball. Two more jugs fall off.

Our CDs are mixed together on the same shelf. Our paychecks go into a joint checking account. We share a lease. A dog named Gus.

Life is easier to *not* sweep the rug out from under it.

Vanessa took me back. And I promised her it would never happen again. From that moment on, I'm just like our park bench—bolted into the concrete. Not going anywhere.

Besides, how bad of a guy would I be if I hurt her like that a second time?

My father once gave me advice when I asked him about relationships. About when you know you've found the right one. When to check out of the game and settle down.

He told me, "If life hands you lemons, then that means you'll never have to drink orange juice."

He told me this while drinking a glass of iced tea, so to this day, I still don't know what he was trying to tell me.

I throw the last ball at the two remaining jugs, knocking off only one.

Six out of seven wins a pocket-size yellow teddy bear.

The kid hands me the consolation prize, and I hold it out to the girl next to me.

"I can't accept this." She stares down at it between us, not grabbing it. "But I'm quite sure you have someone else you can give it to."

I watch her boyfriend walk out of the bathroom, and the two of them walk away from me down the park, hand in hand.

As they make their way through the crowd, I hear her say to him, "Honey, did you know that Lake Erie is the shallowest of all the Great Lakes?"

I didn't tell her the rest of that piece of trivia. By having less water, the lake gets warm in the summer, but extremely cold in the winter. The lake freezes quickly, with over 70 percent of the lake covered in ice. All winter long, under the ice, a toxic blanket of green algae forms. It often grows over one hundred miles in size, and the algae suck oxygen from the water, killing off much of the fish and plant life underneath. As the algae die off each year, they sink to the bottom of the lake, creating a dead zone.

I turn back to the kid in the tent, handing him another five dollars. "Let me play again."

The sun is just about to set over the horizon, nothing but hazy blue, choppy water which looks murky gray, with shades of green algae already starting to show through.

Vanessa will be sitting at our bench, waiting for me to come back. And I will go back, because I promised her.

The kid hands me three balls.

Four-foot-tall. Neon-pink. Stuffed elephant. It's the grand prize that sits on the top shelf, just out of our reach. It catches our eyes as we pass by, and we decide we want to stop and win it, believing it will bring us joy, even if for only a fleeting moment in time, before it ends up on the curb, and we forget we ever had it in the first place.

But I still cock my arm back and throw the ball as hard as I can toward that stack of jugs across the tent.

Harnessing Big Data

On her way to the sex-toy shop, Beth bumped into Hugh and his family.

What were the odds? She was rarely on Mercer Street and had quickly stepped into a store to warm up for a moment after the chilly walk from the Spring Street subway station. Holiday shoppers were cluttering up the narrow streets and knocking into each other with their oversized gift bags.

It was a Kate Spade store. There was Hugh in front of her, looking baffled, windblown, encased in a puffy parka, staring at her blankly as if trying to place her in the universe. They sat next to each other twelve hours a day, Monday through Friday, in an open office on Park Avenue. But here she was, out of context. A saleswoman walked by and admired Beth's coat. "I love that purple."

"Oh, thank you." Beth smiled and then said "Hello" to Hugh. His two bored, blonde teen-aged daughters glanced at her as Hugh introduced them. His wife wandered over from another section of the store and smiled genuinely at her.

"We've all been *deathly* ill for the holiday" said Hugh in his clipped British accent. Beth stepped backward.

"No, no we are healed," said the wife with a laugh. Hugh, though, encouraged Beth to be careful and stand apart. Grisly details of the illness were shared: toilet hugging, virus factoids, bathroom floors slept on, etc.

"We thought maybe it was food poisoning," said the wife. Beth calculated when she'd last lunched with Hugh. Was he germy then? Had they eaten anything similar? She deduced it had been two days before the holiday break, so she should be okay.

After their polite good-byes, after her purchases later at Toys at Babeland from an emaciated sales girl with a ring in her nose—who had discussed her clit in more detail than anyone ever had—Beth carefully folded her new items and the brazenly labeled store bag into her eco-friendly sack out of fear she'd once again run into Hugh's clan in the neighborhood.

In a few months, Hugh would be fired and would relocate to a new job in Amsterdam. Beth hung on and on, clinging to her job as if it were a life preserver floating near the Titanic. New bosses appeared and disappeared on a regular basis. The cost of farewell lunches and Papyrus "good luck" cards mounted. Even Eduardo, the shoe man, who came every Thursday to polish the executive's shoes, was going back to Brazil. He was tired and suddenly muddy faced. Beth wished him well, and as she shook his hand and thanked him, he held his other hand to his heart, with tears in his eyes.

Beth signed up for free webinars to try to update her skills and understand the fury to harness big data—all the rage. She attended meetings where her "superiors" overused the words "cadence" and "sticky" and brayed phrases like "let's not boil the ocean." Metrics were everywhere, measuring things no one cared about but that looked impressive on a PowerPoint slide.

On the webinars, Beth would get distracted by the multiple messages invading her computer screen: join the conversation; chat; join the call; multiple attendees are typing; press *1 on your phone, or use chat below right. She was exhausted by the nonstop commands and could barely concentrate on the webinar's content. It was like a demanding religion. There were so many rules of participation.

She helped Hugh's replacement choose his executive photo for the org chart. Little squares of Jerry multiplied endlessly across the page. They all looked demented, artificial, and the same. Jerry forced his introverted cheek muscles in an unnatural effort to smile, something Jerry never did in real life. Or at real work anyway.

Jerry had recently told Beth that a picture of her at a team building meeting, where her colleague had his arm around her and a deflated basketball on his head, could be used at her wake or retirement party, whichever came first.

"There'll be neither," Beth said.

"Oh?" Jerry seemed surprised and returned to his spreadsheet of data. Jerry had a webfoot, which, like the details of Hugh's family virus, was too much data for Beth. She didn't want to visualize any part of Jerry's body, including his feet. Feet he apparently planned to walk on to her nonexistent wake. Although who's to say her nonexistent wake would occur before Jerry's?

Statistically speaking, big data would propose hers would occur first. But she was siding with Albert Einstein who once said, "Not everything that can be counted counts, and not everything that counts can be counted." She wasn't convinced big data could solve the mysteries of the universe, fix the economy, or find the Malaysian jetliner.

Where did the expression "who's to say" come from anyway, Beth wondered? That was a piece of big data she'd find interesting and useful.

At the early morning introductions at the team building meeting, Beth confidently took the microphone when it was handed to her. She stared a moment at the tense, tired faces in the room. For a moment, she considered singing a song to break the ice and wake (or at least slightly cheer) everyone up. *A little song, a little dance, a little seltzer in your pants.* But would they recognize any song she chose to sing? Instead, she returned to business; she was data-centric, not eccentric, in her remarks. When she finished, the meeting facilitator joked how comfortable Beth seemed with the mic, unlike everyone else.

A deep-voiced statistician at the meeting talked about the "level of missingness" from their employee engagement survey. It occurs, he explained, when survey information is not completed; it confounds the stat guys why folks don't answer all the survey questions. Beth thought it was obvious: if no one wants to reply to a particular question, could it shout any louder that this is the problem in the eyes of the employee? And wasn't using the word "engagement" in a work context, as opposed to using it for a euphoric state prior to nuptials, a bit of a stretch? Were employees supposed to be euphoric at work, even in the midst of layoffs?

At the afternoon session, they had to once again talk about their Myers-Briggs scores. This outdated psychological assessment tool, based on Jungian theory, was designed by a mother and daughter. Beth thought this piece of data should immediately disqualify it as a valuable assessment tool. Who's to say any mother-daughter team could assess the human race? Or agree on how to categorize all of humanity? Beth and her mother couldn't agree on breakfast.

Beth had been forced over her long career to take the test multiple times, usually receiving the same score. But she always worried about her results; she knew she had issues with authority. She even had issue with suggestions. But who's to say that's a bad thing?

They showed a scatter diagram of workforce demographics at the meeting.

"See, this is very bad," said their VP. "See this cluster? We have way too many old people. This is a crisis." The VP had a smattering of faint, watercolor green lines smudged on her cheekbone, like delicate etchings on an Easter egg. "Oh," the VP laughed, when out of concern that it was ink or an injury, Beth quietly asked about it during their break, "that's where my dermatologist got a little rough during my monthly injections."

After the meeting, at the team building dinner activity, Beth had an unexpected victory in the Skee-Ball event at Dave & Busters. It required no skill other than realizing that tossing the ball into the circles worth 100 points yielded a higher score than wasting efforts on those only worth 50 points. This, she supposed, was harnessing big data in real time.

Back at the office, a twenty-something on the "wellness" committee asked Beth if she would do a testimonial. "I heard you play tennis regularly, and I think it would be great if someone as senior as you can speak to the benefits of wellness." Beth watched his lips as he continued speaking and inserting the word "senior" every few seconds into the conversation. Beth was confused for a moment whether he was referring to her status at the company but then realized she was inflating her position, and he really was just using a code word for old. "It's so amazing someone as senior as you can exercise regularly! I hope you will consider it, doing a testimonial." Beth sighed and mumbled, "We'll see."

Maybe instead she could do a testimonial on her unexpected Skee-Ball victory. It had pleased her to beat all her surprised younger colleagues, even if it was an insipid activity and her progressive eyeglasses had hampered her in the basketball challenge.

Who's to say that an invisible, older worker like Beth—whose gynecologist had filled out a sex-toys prescription for her (things were closing up); whose Myers-Briggs score had suddenly shifted (perhaps as a result of trying to survive in the face of corporate downsizing) from years of charmingly matching Nelson Mandela's score to being a dead ringer for the inhumane Steve Jobs and Margaret Thatcher (even though Beth doubted any of them had actually taken the survey); who had recently been stopped on the street by a stranger who insisted she would benefit from collagen and eye serum ("Do you sleep on the left side?" he'd asked. "Your face is so flat there."); who had never even been to Amsterdam; who had her own level of missingness in grasping the need for nonstop fucking data—who's to say she couldn't successfully and repeatedly (with glorious stickiness and cadence) toss a grimy round object up lanes into ridiculous concentric circles and KICK BUTT at Skee-Ball? Who's to say that couldn't be memorialized by a testimonial, along with the deflated basketball head photo, to convince the company she was skilled, ready to take on anything thrown at her: an Iron lady, competitive, metrics-savvy, engaged, and fun?

Who's to say? Not Beth.

Yesterday I Had the Hiccups

I am allergic to being ignored.
Please scratch my itches
before I tip-toe
back and forth along the bluff
and find delight in
my own compulsion to repeat.
It's a sure bet I'll retaliate
and grouse a regrettable phrase.
Down the fire road on the left,
where the horse flies lie in wait,
one's personality is downgraded
to a debtors' prison.

After all is said and done,
there is still more to do.
Events jolt:
they overawe all patterns,
only to be "processed,"
squeezed into a jack in the box.
We have therapy to thank for that.
A speech act is also a hiccup.
And vice versa, my darling.

I mime Sisyphus--
A voice told me that somewhere uphill
I might find an antidote
to the venom in your wordlessness.

John Ballantine

I Lost My Voice, Driving

I lost my voice on the New Jersey Turnpike between exit 14 and 13 on October 10, 1967, to be precise, or so I thought, but looking back, it was not my voice. It was sculptured, molded, and shaped by eighteen years of schooling. "What are the causes of the Civil War, why did Lady Macbeth feel so bad, and was Benedict Arnold really the traitor they thought he was?"

"Foul, foul, double trouble, see Birnam Wood stir. All is not as it seems."

I wrote essays and took to quantum mechanics with a passion— "God would not play dice with the universe"—only Caesar's Gallic wars and Aeneid's wanderings left me flat. My eyes saw more than these words, formed over centuries. My lean body, all 6 feet 1 inch with sandy blond hair, showed the privilege of class that I barely understood.

I thought I had a voice. My understanding of the world carried me this far: Good family, very good schools, a path to prosperity, wife, home, children, and maybe a picket fence. You know, the *Leave it to Beaver* neighborhood just down the street. This was America before the Vietnam War, Civil Rights, *The Feminine Mystique*, poverty, and the Cold War. A world I barely saw on the New Jersey Turnpike with trucks crashing down on the blue MG, as my father told me that he and my mother were separating.

"What, what did you say?" over the deafening din of cars roaring by.

"Your mother and I will not live together at 82 Library Place this year. I have a basement apartment near school in Hoboken."

A city I never saw. I heard my father speak, but I went quiet and looked at the planes sliding into Newark airport.

"What you, you didn't know? How could you not know?"

I had no idea. I did not know my mother and dad as separate

people. I looked at the tachometer spinning above 4,000 revolutions per minute, trying to keep up with the trucks looming above. The planes crossed the highway, close enough to see the passengers looking down on us. I took People's Express from Boston at 9:00 a.m. that morning, two weeks into my freshman year, summoned home for this? What were they thinking?

The October day was graying. Here I was on Saturday morning, visiting my broken home in Princeton, New Jersey. I looked again at the dashboard. I guess these are the facts. My parents are separated. I had no idea what that meant. The noise of the road subsided as we passed Elizabeth, New Jersey, and the Mobil refinery on the right, flaring off the gas.

I still didn't know what to say. This was not some sort of Greek tragedy, with a chorus whispering directions. Just me and my distracted father who was trying to assure me that everything was okay. What did that mean?

"They didn't know what to say, what to do. Divorce didn't happen back then."

"We will have Thanksgiving together and not tell our neighbors or our friends what is happening. I will sleep on the third floor and, over Christmas, we will fly to Minneapolis to talk with your grandparents. Then we'll take the train to Montana for a week of skiing with your cousins. That is the right time to explain the separation to Mumps and Gumps." This was such a logical, doable plan for them, my parents.

I didn't lose my voice then, because I had no such voice. No words for the emotions stirring beneath. No worries about the relationships I didn't understand. If somebody didn't like me, "tant pis." It must mean I am doing something right. I am here. Noticed, not liked, so what?

Love in the books, in lines of poetry, was about conquest, miscommunication, and not understanding. Often something worked out, or they died of sorrow. And love, not marriage, was mostly about sex, not attained. That is what they said in the books I read.

So I had no voice, no words for the slowing tachometer as we got off at exit 9 and made our way down Route 1 to Princeton. "How are classes—astronomy, Greek tragedy, history of revolutions, the renaissance, and Chinese dynasties? What do you like?"

"Oh, you know, just the same. Sit, read, take notes, write papers, and talk to people in the Harvard Union at dinner. Rugby too, with the future King of Togo, a big round burly fellow." I looked blankly out at the cut down cornfields lining the road.

We drove down Nassau Street, turned right on Library Place, and parked by the back porch, entering the kitchen, not the front door. The kitchen was warm, with apple pie, fried chicken, and hugs. But my mother was not right and, Chia, my younger sister by twenty-three months, was uncomfortable—she did not like this meal because she knew all along, for months, and she didn't tell me. Henrietta too did not smile easily as she cooked our meal.

We stood around the tin table in the kitchen, cutting the chicken and eating right there. "All will be the same." My mother's eyes were red, and they looked away as she spoke. My father tried to smile. "We'll have Thanksgiving here, and then you two can join your dad in New York. He will be here for the day, and you and Chia will be with him on Friday for a play."

But that is what my mother did.

I murmured, "Okay." Just accept the facts. What did that mean? I didn't shout, cry, ask why, or look away. Maybe I was a stoic or just out of it. Chia acted as if this was normal, part of life in our home. Of course, we didn't say anything.

"Don't tell anyone. Don't let the Morgensterns, our neighbors, know or your roommate, Mark Jacobs, your best friend from Princeton."

I stood there next to Chia, and we looked at each other, "Okay, but why?"

"It could all work out."

Right. After six years of growing apart, it would not work out. But they didn't know that then.

"Just say no, look away, say nothing, and it will go away. Say no, all will be okay."

I didn't have a voice for this talk. I didn't even know what this scene in the kitchen meant. The world had changed, just like that, on the New Jersey Turnpike with trucks crashing down on me and planes landing one by one, every minute.

~~~

Back in Harvard Yard that Columbus Day, the ROTC was barred from recruiting. Protestors stormed the halls in Columbia, and the war was on TV. Bob Dylan told us, beware the "Masters of War." I hovered in the dark rooms with my friends, listened to the music, looked at the windows, and said little.

The voice that I wore so well that grew over eighteen years failed me. I had been taught with the careful instruction of schoolmasters these words and these sentences, but they did not make sense as October darkened into November. My world was not right.

"The answer, my friend, is blowin' in the wind."

Bruce Bagnell

Love Letters

in knowing you
I search,
finding their love letters
under your bed,
voices silent,
old pieces of dried paper
upon which we will rain
the splinters of the bed stays
and drown as we liquefy the walls
until their pulp is washed away, gone.

My Eskimo Brother

Nobody ever listens to me.

I say no, absolutely not. But that doesn't stop roommate Mark. That doesn't stop roommate Mark and his buddy Trey (my Eskimo brother) from rearranging the living conditions. Doesn't stop them from spoiling my new romance. No, Mark invites Trey (my Eskimo brother) to move right on in.

He says, look, there is plenty of space in here, holding open the small, half-sized door leading into the darkness under our stairs. And Trey (my Eskimo brother) nods happily and shuffles in with duffel bags slung over each shoulder.

At nights I can hear him, rustling around, thumping elbows and knees because it's a cramped crawl space between my and Mark's rooms.

But the noise is not the *real* problem, only part of it.

My new girl Madelyn is my main concern.

My new girl Madelyn with her long legs she stretches out in the sand and the sun and how warm they are to touch, to slowly rub. Her long blonde hair and two-piece suits. The way she says mine, mine, paddling ahead on the beginning of a slowly approaching wave, swelling. The way she hops right up, drops hard right toward the pier cutting the tail back, spraying salt water in the air. And her in the reflection of the sun through each tiny droplet, each individual soul separated from the body of the ocean, from nature, makes her glow like life resurrected.

But Madelyn won't come over. Not anymore.

This is how it's put:

How would you like it, she asks, having to hear your old flame with a new flame, hearing the sounds of breathing and creaking through cracks in the thin walls.

And I didn't like knowing he'd been there before, him in her or her on him, moving bodies in time, sweating, kissing lips and tangled limbs. But that was our bond, Trey and I, our brotherhood through my new girl.

I go to tell my landlord about all of this.

She listens and blows grey smoke while grimly buttering a sandwich roll. I explained, There's a runaway drug-dealer holed up in our crawlspace who just so happens to be my Eskimo brother and now my new girl Madelyn won't come over and it's all Mark's fault.

Mark, she said spitting out tobacco flakes from her hand rolled cigarette.

She tosses me a padlock. This has happened before, she says.

What?

That boy under the stairs,

Trey, I say (my Eskimo brother).

Whatever, she said, I call this the Lock Box, clamp that on for a few days he won't last long. And when it's over, he'll happily walk out your door.

I invite Madelyn over and tell her everything is taken care of. She comes.

Together, in twisted, tousled sheets, lying fast-heart-beating on our backs.

I look at a small patch of peach on her soft cheek and tell her about how I love...

She cuts me off, shaking her head, infatuation she says, I've seen this all before. And cool humid air through the window is our silence, forever, before it's broken by the wild thrashing and clamoring under the stairs, now sounding more panicked more desperate than ever before.

Cooking By Flashlight, Supper By Lantern
(With Loons)

Symes Pond, Vermont

The heat had parboiled us for three days,
    strawberry flies had chewed our don't-DEET-on-me skin,
        mosquitoes had sung because I call the wheezy scree

that scuttled us from the porch *song* so the planet's
    self-evident simmering doesn't slap a stick of dynamite
        in my right hand, snap my left thumbnail cross the tip

of a strike-anywhere match & frog-march my sweat-slick,
    metonymic ass toward the nearest oligarch juggling
        last winter's snowballs as he sniggers at all us

book-reading Poindexters. That son of a bitch has no idea
    my love of lyrical anthropomorphism has delivered him up
        to a post-prandial lemon vodka, has freed him to float

in the current burbling through his earbuds
    —a think-tank "audio-book" pooh-poohing
        the Battle of the Overpass perhaps—

& oozing past the tweezed pinna into his skull,
    suffusing the brain-stuff with soothing
        abstraction, safe as George Will's adoration

of baseball. Rain poured down at last.
    We drove north cool & dry, remarking
        the devastation, reciting our gratitude

for where & how we found ourselves.
    All up Route 5, downed power lines,
        tree limbs, impromptu cataracts,

rescue vehicles careening & near the turn
    onto the two-track that would lead us home,
        a platoon of citizens chainsawing a hemlock

off the collapsed roof of a sagging farmhouse
    cut up into apartments. The further back
        into the woods we drove, the worse it got,

rain overwhelming the wipers, steam condensing
    on all the windows & two miles in, an oak down
        & it wasn't home we headed for except *home*

means wherever we three find ourselves.
    We slogged down & failed to budge
        the tree, shouting our failure & mucking back

to the car to call Carl, who came awhile later
    to saw the tree up & follow us to the cabin
        to light the lanterns & point out the gas line.

All week, our son had mimicked the loons,
    but not that night. He shone the flashlight
        he & he alone had remembered to bring

on the cast-iron pan his parents filled
    with the feast. A cool, wet breeze wafted in.
        We'd earned the right to employ the word *wafted*

& to thank the Lord of Hosts for the nearby
    cell-phone tower & chainsaws & gasoline
        & the air-conditioning for which we didn't hunger

that night, the bullfrogs being bullfrogs & the bats bats.

AUTHORS

Bruce Bagnell

After Bruce received his bachelor's in English from Fairleigh Dickinson University, he went on to earn a master's from John F. Kennedy University. Throughout the years he has worked as a cook, mechanic, and college professor; held various management positions; and was a USAF captain in Vietnam. Now retired, Bruce focuses wholeheartedly on his writing and has been published in *OmniVerse, The Scribbler, The Round, Blue Lake Review, Chaparrel, Oxford Magazine, Diverse Voices Quartery, Studio1, Westview Magazine, and The Alembic.* He also hosts at Poetry Express Berkeley and edits their on-line publication PoeBerkMag. Bruce is a member of the Bay Area Poets Coalition and has twice been awarded honorable mention in their Maggi H. Meyer Memorial Poetry Contest.

John Ballantine

John Ballantine is a professor at Brandeis International Business School. He teaches courses in economics, finance and energy and is director of a one year program in finance. John received his bachelor degree in English from Harvard University and master's degree and Ph.D. from University of Chicago and NYU, respectively. He has been writing on the side for many years. Over the past five years, John has been part of weekly "Writing Down the Bones," Natalie Goldberg's writing group in Concord, Ma. where free form writing practices and creativity are encouraged. His recent reflections and memoir vignettes are an outgrowth of the voice that emerged from these writing classes. John continues to make time for writing, reading and discovering our wonderful complex world while teaching full complement of classes at Brandeis.

Vincent Barry

Vincent Barry's affection for creative writing is rooted in the theatre. More years ago than he prefers to remember, his one-act plays caught the attention of the late Arthur Ballet at the University of Minnesota's Office for Advanced Drama Research and Wynn Handman at New York's The American Place Theatre. Some productions followed, as well as a residency at The Edward Albee Foundation on Long Island. Meanwhile, Barry was teaching philosophy at Bakersfield College in California and authoring philosophy textbooks. Now retired from teaching, he has returned to fiction. Besides *Crack the Spine*, his stories have appeared in *Writing Tomorrow Magazine* ("Dear Fellow Californian," June 2014), *The Write Room* ("When It First Came Out," Fall 2014), and *Blue Lake Review* ("The Girl with the Sunflower Yellow Hot Rod Limo," December 2014).

Keith Buie

Keith Buie lives in Cleveland, Ohio. His work has appeared in *Burnt Tongues*, the award-winning (This is Horror) and Bram Stoker-nominated anthology edited by best-selling author Chuck Palahniuk. His work has also appeared in *Eleven Eleven, The MacGuffin, Natural Bridge, Pisgah Review, Quiddity International Literary Journal, Rio Grande Review, Willard & Maple,* and *Metal Scratches.* Keith is currently writing his first novel. He is represented by Elizabeth Winick Rubinstein of McIntosh & Otis, Inc. Literary Agency.

Dusty Cooper

Dusty is writing a collection of stories based on his experiences in the Gulf of Thailand and a novel expanding his story "Conditioning a Wolf." His work has appeared in *Weave Magazine, Crack the Spine, Berkeley Fiction Review, Bartleby Snopes, Paper Nautilus,* and *Litro.* Dusty is an instructor at Southeastern Louisiana University.

Daniel Davis

Daniel Davis is the Nonfiction Editor for The Prompt Literary Magazine. His own work has appeared in various online and print journals. You can find him on Facebook and Twitter.

Nancy Ford Dugan

Nancy Ford Dugan's work has been nominated for a Pushcart Prize (in 2012 and 2013) and has been published in *Blue Lake Review, Cimarron Review, Passages North, The Minnesota Review, The Alembic, Euphony, Lullwater Review, The Battered Suitcase, The MacGuffin, Epiphany, Coe Review, Buffalo Carp, Delmarva Review, Desert Voices, The Dirty Goat, The Doctor T.J. Eckleburg Review, The Hurricane Review, The Old Red Kimono, RiverSedge, Superstition Review, Schuylkill Valley Journal, Words and Images, Tin House's Open Bar, The Writer's Post Journal*, and *Eastern Shore Savvy*. She lives in New York City and previously resided in Michigan, Ohio, and Washington, DC.

Gwendolyn Edward

Gwendolyn Edward writes fiction, poetry, and nonfiction. Her magical realism, slip stream, and fabulist short stories have been accepted by *Crack the Spine, Bourbon Penn, Jersey Devil Press, Jenny, Lightning Cake, The Copperfield Review*, and others. She retains a MA in Creative Writing from the University of North Texas and is currently pursuing a MFA at Bennington. She works with *Fifth Wednesday Journal* as an assistant non-fiction editor and also teaches Creative Writing.

Priscilla Frake

Priscilla Frake's first full-length book of poetry, "Correspondence," was published in 2013 by *Mutabilis Press*. In 2012, she won the*Lorene Pouncey Award* at the Houston Poetry Fest and was nominated for a Pushcart Prize. Her work has appeared in many journals including *Nimrod, Atlanta Review, The Sow's Ear Poetry Review, The Carolina Quarterly, The Spoon River Poetry Review*, and *The Midwest Quarterly*.

Catherine Gonick

Catherine Gonick's poetry has appeared or is forthcoming in publications including *Boston Review, Pivot, Crack the Spine, Ginosko, Word Riot, Amarillo Bay, Forge, Sukoon. Soul-Lit, Jet Fuel Review*, and *Jewish Women's Literary Annual*. She was awarded the Ina Coolbrith Memorial

Prize for Poetry as an undergraduate at U.C. Berkeley and completed an MA in creative writing at the City University of New York. She is the author of produced plays and was a finalist in the National Ten-Minute Play Contest with the Actors Theatre of Louisville. As part of a startup company that turns organic waste into clean, sustainable energy, she divides her time between New York and California.

Ken Haas

Ken Haas lives in San Francisco, where he works in healthcare and sponsors a poetry writing program at the UCSF Children's Hospital. His poems have appeared or are forthcoming in *Alabama Literary Review, Amarillo Bay, Caesura, The Cape Rock, Cottonwood, Existere, Forge, The Coachella Review, Freshwater, Hawai'i Pacific Review, Helix, Lullwater Review, Moon City Review, Natural Bridge, Pennsylvania English, Pigsah Review, Quiddity, Red Wheelbarrow, Rougarou, Salthill Journal, Schuylkill Valley Journal Of The Arts, Spoon River Poetry Review, Squaw Valley Review, Stickman Review, Tattoo Highway,* and *Wild Violet*. His work has also been anthologized in *The Place That Inhabits Us* (Sixteen Rivers Press, 2010) and the *Marin Poetry Center Anthology* (2012, 2013).

Dennis Scott Herbert

Dennis Scott Herbert is dangerous. He is a current MFA candidate at Minnesota State University, Mankato where he hosts the Writer's Bloc Reading Series and serves as fiction editor for the *Blue Earth Review*. His work has appeared in *Hobart, Cardinal Sins, Jet Fuel Review,* and *Tampa Review Online*.

Karen Hildebrand

Karen Hildebrand is chief content officer for the New York-based publisher of *Dance Magazine*. Her play, "The Old In and Out," cowritten with poet Madeline Artenberg, was produced off-off Broadway by Three Rooms Press in 2013.

Garrett Hines

Garrett Hines was born in New Orleans, Louisiana. He's a graduate of Southeastern Louisiana University, where he received a Bachelor' Degree in English, and a Master's Degree in Creative Writing. Other publications include *The Gambit Literary Journal* and *Louisiana Road Trips Magazine*. He has also been a panelist at the *Tennessee Williams Literary Festival* in New Orleans. Garrett currently lives in Los Angeles, California.

Lynn Hoggard

Translator and poet Lynn Hoggard has published five books and hundreds of articles, poems, and reviews. Her translation of Nelida, a novel by Marie d'Agoult (companion of Franz Liszt), won the 2003 Soeurette Diehl Fraser Award for Best Translation given by the Texas Institute of Letters. A resident of Wichita Falls, TX, her most recent book is a memoir, Motherland, Stories and Poems from Louisiana (May 2014, Lamar University Press). In her view, poems express meanings implicit in the visible world.

M. David Hornbuckle

M. David Hornbuckle is the author of a novel, "Zen Mississippi," and a collection of short stories, "The Salvation of Billy Wayne Carter". His fiction, poetry, and articles have been published in more than thirty journals. Currently, he lives in Birmingham, Alabama, where he teaches English at the local university. He is also the Managing Editor of the *Steel Toe Review* and the *Birmingham Free Press*.

J. Edward Kruft

J. Edward Kruft received his MFA in fiction writing from Brooklyn College. His stories have appeared in Bartleby Snopes, Bop Dead City, Eunoia Review, and Soundings Review. He grew up on the coast of Washington state where, in high school, he drove a '76 Chevy Nova hatchback named Izzy. He now lives in Astoria, NY and Asbury Park,

NJ with his husband, Mike, and their Keeshond-mix rescue, Aine, and drives an unnamed Volvo.

Marie Lecrivain

Marie Lecrivain is the edtior-publisher of *poeticdiversity: the litzine of Los Angeles*, a photographer, and a writer-in-residence at her apartment. She's been published in various journals, including *Non-Binary Review, Edgar Allan Poetry Journal*, and *Poetry Salzburg Review*. Her newest book, "The Virtual Tablet of Irma Tre" (copyright 2014 *Edgar & Lenore's Publishing House*), a series of alchemical poems, is available through Amazon.com.

Robert McKean

"I have had stories published in *The Kenyon Review, The Chicago Review, Dublin Quarterly, The MacGuffin, The Bacon Review, Ruminate, Front Range Review, 34th Parallel, Crack the Spine, Armchair/Shotgun* (forthcoming), and elsewhere. My collection of stories was a Finalist in the Flannery O'Connor Award for Short Fiction and the Mary McCarthy Prize in Short Fiction. A novel I am working on was a Semi-Finalist in the Peter Taylor Prize for the Novel. I have been awarded a Massachusetts Artist's Grant for my fiction."

Edward D. Miller

Edward D. Miller's poetry appears appears in *Counterexample Poetics, Hinchas de Poesia, Wilderness House Literary Journal, The Boston Literary Magazine*, and *Red Fez*. He teaches media and film at the City University of New York.

Christopher Ozog

Christopher Ozog is a 23 year old writer who resides in Ann Arbor, Michigan. His work has previously appeared in *Burningword, The Commonline*, and *Crack the Spine's* digital issue.

John Repp

John Repp's fourth collection of poetry, *Fat Jersey Blues*, won the 2013 Akron Poetry Prize from the University of Akron Press.

Ron Riekki

Ron Riekki's books include "U.P." (*Ghost Road Press*) and "The Way North: Collected Upper Peninsula New Works" (*Wayne State University Press*, chosen by the Library of Michigan as a 2014 Michigan Notable Book). May 2015, Michigan State University Press publishes "Here: Women Writing Michigan's Upper Peninsula." His plays include "All Saints' Day" (*Ruckus Theater*), "Dandelion Cottage" (*Lake Superior Theatre*), and "Carol" (*equity production, Stageworks/Hudson*).

Saudamini Siegrist

Saudamini Siegrist was born in Montana and grew up in the West and Midwest. She earned a doctorate in English literature at NYU and a master's in poetry at Columbia, and has taught at St. John's University and at Fordham University. Her work has appeared or is forthcoming in Forge, Salamander, Free State Review, Studio One, The Worcester Review, The North Stone Review, Zone 3 and Al-Raida Journal and received a nomination for the Pushcart Prize. She currently lives in New York City and works at UNICEF on human rights and humanitarian action.

Patty Somlo

Patty Somlo has received four Pushcart Prize nominations and one nomination for storySouth's Million Writers Award, as well as having an essay selected as a Notable for Best American Essays 2014. Her second book, *Hairway to Heaven Stories*, which will include "Horn Man," is forthcoming in January 2017 from Cherry Castle Publishing.

T.A. Stanley

T. A. Stanley lives in Brooklyn where she is attending NYU as a graduate student with a focus on Gender Politics. She is currently working on a series of short fiction pieces in which uses magical and fantastic elements to illuminate how the lived experience of "womanhood" has made her feel through embodiments of these emotions in surreal acts and transformations. Her work also has appeared in Belleville Park Pages, See Spot Run Literary Magazine, CircleShow, Vagabonds: Anthology of the Mad Ones, and The Atlas Review.

Lisa C. Taylor

Lisa C. Taylor is the author of four poetry collections. Her upcoming debut collection of short fiction, *Growing a New Tail* will be published in 2015. Lisa teaches creative writing at a small college. She enjoys reading her work in unusual places and so far has read at a gourmet food shop, a carwash, an Italian restaurant, and a beauty parlor. She aspires to read her work on a train.

Dvorah Telushkin

Between 1975-1988 Dvorah Telushkin worked as a personal assistant, editor, and translator for Isaac Bashevis Singer, the Yiddish writer who won the 1978 Nobel Prize in Literature. Her translations appeared in *The New Yorker*, and in collections of Mr. Singer's stories published by *Farrar Straus and Giroux.* In 1997, she published her memoir, "Master of Dreams," telling the story of her twelve-year apprenticeship with Mr. Singer. The book received wide critical attention, including a review in *The New York Times. The Weekly Standard* called the book "a fully realized portrait of a writer... a reminder that the author's life was as fascinating as his best fiction." She is currently completing her first novel, "The Cry of the Loon." In addition, she has recently completed a one-woman show, In*Search of the Perfect Pocketbook*, which is currently being launched. In 2013, she published in the poetry journals, "The Light Ekphrastic", "Literary Juice", and "Orion Headless."

Daniel W. Thompson

Daniel W. Thompson's fiction has appeared recently or is forthcoming at publications like *Bartleby Snopes, Jersey Devil Press, Literary Orphans, decomP*, and *Spartan*. As a child, his grandfather paid him $5 an hour to clean up frozen cow patties and pull stones out of the vegetable garden. Now he lives in downtown Richmond, VA with his wife and daughter cleaning up diapers and dog fur – no compensation has been offered.

Judith Thompson

As an emerging voice in the Taos poetry scene, Judith has been involved in several curated ekphrasis events and has aired on KVOT, a local radio station. She was also selected to read at the Society of The Muse of the Southwest (SOMOS) poetry series. From 2008–2012, Judith was enrolled in a poetry workshop with Sawnie Morris, and in 2009 she studied with Dana Levin in *A Room Of Her Own Foundation's* poetry intensive. Her work has appeared in the *Taos Journal of International Poetry* and *Art and HOWL: The Voice of UNM Taos*. A classically trained musician, Judith received her bachelor's in music from Occidental College and, before retiring early, worked as a symphony orchestra executive. For fourteen years, Judith and her husband lived aboard a forty-foot sailboat. Now that they have come ashore, she finds passion in growing organic vegetables and fruits when she's not immersed in reading and writing poetry.

Melissa Tombro

Melissa Tombro is an Associate Professor at the Fashion Institute of Technology, SUNY, in New York City, where she teaches writing. In addition to teaching, she volunteers for the New York Writers Coalition, where she runs writing workshops for at-risk and underserved populations. She lives in Sunset Park, Brooklyn, with her husband Matt and their dog Lily. Her work appeared in *Eclectica* magazine.

Ani Tuzman

Ani Tuzman is a writing mentor at *Dance of the Letters Writing Center* that she founded in 1982 to help children, teens, and adults experience the joys of writing. Years earlier, before leaving city life, she also cofounded *A Kangaroo's Pouch* (El Buche del Canguro), a bilingual and multicultural school in the Boston area. Ani's work has been published in *CALYX, Mothering, Tikkun, Sanctuary, Darshan, FamilyFun*, and *Body Mind Spirit,* among other journals and magazines. Her writing is included in such anthologies as "Chicken Soup For The Mother & Daughter Soul," "Divine Mosaic," and *MotherPoet*. Her poetry is also featured on two CDs, "Spirals Of Light" and "Poetry and Chamber Music on Themes Of The Holocaust." She has received the Anna Davidson Rosenberg Prize for Poems on the Jewish Experience and the Peter K. Hixson Memorial Award for Creative Writers.

This anthology is generously sponsored by Outskirts Press

Visit www.crackthespine.com to subscribe to our weekly digital magazine or to review our submission guidelines.

www.ingramcontent.com/pod-product-compliance
Lightning Source LLC
Chambersburg PA
CBHW070555180626
46817CB00005B/1844